The Reagan
Strategic Defense Initiative

The Reagan Strategic Defense Initiative: A Technical, Political, and Arms Control Assessment

by

Sidney D. Drell, Philip J. Farley, and David Holloway
Center for International Security and Arms Control
Stanford University

BALLINGER PUBLISHING COMPANY
Cambridge, Massachusetts
A Subsidiary of Harper & Row, Publishers, Inc.

The International Strategic Institute at Stanford (ISIS) administers two affiliated programs: the Center for International Security and Arms Control and the Northeast Asia-United States Forum on International Policy. Both the Center and the Forum bring together Stanford University faculty members from several scholarly disciplines with senior specialists from around the world for research projects, seminars and conferences, and international scholarly exchange. They both sponsor extensive publications, including Occasional Papers, Special Reports, and Research Notes. The Center and the Forum also publish through Stanford University Press *ISIS Studies in International Security and Arms Control* and *ISIS Studies in International Policy*.

International Standard Book Number: 0-88730-064-2

Library of Congress Catalog Card Number: 85-3916

Printed in the United States of America

Library of Congress Cataloging in Publication Data

Drell, Sidney D. (Sidney David), 1926-
  The Reagan strategic defense initiative.

  Originally published: Stanford, Calif.: International Strategic Institute at Stanford, c1984.
  Includes bibliographical references and index.
  1. Ballistic missile defenses—United States. 2. United States—Military policy. I. Farley, Philip J., 1916-   . II. Holloway, David, 1943-
III. Title.
UG743.D74 1985 358'.17'0973 85-3916
ISBN 0-88730-064-2

Contents

Preface   vii

Acknowledgments   xi

Glossary of Acronyms   xiii

Section I: Introduction   1

Section II: The ABM Treaty and the U.S.-Soviet Strategic Relationship   7

    The ABM Treaty   7

    Soviet Perspectives on the ABM Treaty   13

    The ABM Treaty and the Stability of the U.S.-Soviet Strategic Relationship   29

Section III: The SDI and Its Implications for the U.S.-Soviet Strategic Relationship   39

    The SDI: A Technical Appraisal   39

    The SDI: Possible Outcomes and Their Implications for Deterrence and Stability   64

    The SDI: Allies and Third Countries   74

Section IV: Enhancing Stability and Arms Control Prospects under ABM Limitations   81

Section V: What Should We do? Conclusions and Recommendations   93

    Conclusions   93

    Recommendations   98

(continued)

Appendices

A. The Conclusion of President Reagan's Speech on Defense
   Spending and Defensive Technology, March 23, 1983   101

B. Excerpt from General Secretary Andropov's Interview on
   U.S. Military Policy, March 27, 1983   105

C. Statement on the President's Strategic Defense Initiative
   by the Honorable Richard D. DeLauer   107

D. Treaty Between the United States of America and the
   Union of Soviet Socialist Republics on the Limitation
   of Anti-Ballistic Missile Systems   117

   Agreed Statements, Common Understandings, and
   Unilateral Statements Regarding the Treaty   123

   Protocol to the Treaty   129

E. Allies and Friends Under a Strategic Defense Regime:
   The Asian Connection
   John W. Lewis   133

Index   143

About the Authors   149

Members, Center for International Security and Arms Control,
Stanford University   151

Preface

This study of President Reagan's Strategic Defense Initiative (SDI) was first issued in July 1984 by the Center for International Security and Arms Control at Stanford University. Now that it is being published by the Ballinger Publishing Company, we have the opportunity to ask whether our technical, political, and arms control assessment of the SDI should be changed in the light of developments over the last seven months.

The Reagan Administration remains committed to the Strategic Defense Initiative. The President has several times reaffirmed the purpose he expressed in his speech of March 23, 1983. In his inaugural address on January 21, 1985, for example, he described the SDI as a "research program to find, if we can, a security shield that will destroy nuclear missiles before they reach their target." Such a shield, he said, "would render nuclear weapons obsolete." Other statements by the Administration, however, have defined the goal of the SDI more modestly. *The President's Strategic Defense Initiative,* a document which was issued by the Administration in January 1985 to explain the SDI, states that "providing a better, more stable basis for enhanced deterrence is the central purpose of the SDI program."*

We see no need to amend the technical analysis in this report. Nobody now knows how to build a perfect defense against ballistic missiles, and there is general agreement that total defense against an unconstrained offense is impracticable. Heated debates have taken place about the size of the constellations of space-based battle stations needed to engage an enemy attack, but this is a peripheral issue, and much less significant than the operational problems that a fully integrated system would face in dealing with an offense that could develop and deploy diverse and effective countermeasures.

The Administration has stressed that the SDI program is designed to generate "technologically feasible defense options" and has placed special

* *The President's Strategic Defense Initiative* (Washington D.C.: USGPO, 1985), p. 3.

vii

emphasis on finding non-nuclear mechanisms for destroying enemy ballistic missiles. It has requested $3.7 billion for the program for fiscal year 1986, more than double the $1.4 billion appropriated for fiscal year 1985. We do not see any reason to modify our conclusion that appropriate research need not be funded at more than about $2 billion a year. The research program is still far from the stage of requiring technology demonstrations that would challenge the ABM Treaty.

The Administration has emphasized that the SDI is a research program and that it will be consistent with all U.S. treaty obligations, including the ABM Treaty. The Administration has said little, however, about the technology demonstrations that it plans to conduct. These, as we argue in the report, might well contravene the ABM Treaty. It is important, we believe, that compliance with the treaty be monitored by an impartial commission and not by the program sponsors and managers themselves.

Since this report was first published, the United States and the Soviet Union have agreed to resume arms control talks; and space weapons will be one of the three main areas of negotiation. A fundamental difference exists between the two sides on this issue. The United States wants to make the transition to a defense-dominant strategic relationship by sharply reducing offensive forces while deploying ABM defenses. The Soviet Union, on the other hand, regards its ability to retaliate in the event of a U.S. first strike as a basic condition of its own security and has said that it will not reduce offensive forces unless the United States agrees to forgo the testing and deployment of weapons in space. Such an agreement would undermine a key rationale frequently given for the SDI program.

Thus, it is not only technology but also politics that currently stand in the way of moving toward a defense-dominant strategic relationship between the two superpowers. For defenses to be effective, offensive forces will have to be severely limited. Under present circumstances, however, the commitment in principle by one side, at the highest political level, to designing and building ABM defenses will push the other into expanding and upgrading its offensive forces. It is thus a paradox of current superpower rivalry that the effort to build ABM defenses can, and undoubtedly will, undermine the very condition that is needed to ensure that those defenses are effective.

The strong opposition to the SDI exhibited by the Soviet Union has understandably suggested to some Americans that a program so bitterly attacked by the Soviet Union must represent a powerful U.S. security asset—or at least a valuable one for bargaining purposes. However, the fact of Soviet opposition is far less important to the shaping of U.S. policy decisions than the need to take actions that can help to bring the strategic arms race under control and to reduce the risk of nuclear war. It is surely these critical interests that must determine the scope and pace of our SDI program and the role of strategic defense in the renewed strategic arms negotiations.

Americans, citizens and officials alike, must reflect soberly on the question of what is the right course to follow. We continue to believe that our assessment of the issues raised by the SDI is sound and that it can assist those who are weighing the considerations which will shape the content and pace of the U.S. research program and the handling of strategic defense in the imminent negotiations.

S.D.D.
P.J.F.
D.H.
Stanford
February 1985

Acknowledgments

This report was produced as a project of the Center for International Security and Arms Control at Stanford University, an interdisciplinary program devoted to promoting effective and innovative teaching, training, research, and public outreach in the fields of arms control, disarmament, and international security. The Center, which brings together over fifty arms control scholars and practitioners, emphasizes collaboration among specialists with broadly diverse expertise—academic, technical, and negotiating—in its research in arms control and international security, including U.S.-Soviet and U.S.-Asian relations. Center research and publications are made possible by private gifts and by grants from the Ford Foundation, the Columbia Foundation, the William and Flora Hewlett Foundation, the Weingart Foundation, the Carnegie Corporation of New York, and the MacArthur Foundation.

The Center acknowledges with appreciation the support for this study provided by the William and Flora Hewlett Foundation. The authors wish to acknowledge the valuable advice and assistance of David Bernstein, Coit Blacker, Alexander George, Elliott Levinthal, John Lewis, Wolfgang Panofsky, and Condoleezza Rice at Stanford, as well as the very helpful review and constructive criticism of several colleagues outside the University, specifically, David Elliott, Arthur Hausman, Michael May, William Perry, Robin Staffin, and Albert Wheelon. The assistance of Anne Blenman-Hare, Philip Halperin, Rosemary Hamerton-Kelly, and Kent Wisner in preparing the manuscript is especially appreciated. The opinions expressed in the report are those of the authors and do not represent a position of the Center, the University, or any of the reviewers.

Glossary of Acronyms

ABM	anti-ballistic missile (defense)
ALCM	air-launched cruise missile
AOA	airborne optical adjunct
ASAT	antisatellite (weapons)
ATM	anti-tactical ballistic missile
BMD	ballistic missile defense (i.e., defense of ICBMs by ABM)
DARPA	Defense Advanced Research Projects Agency
DOD	Department of Defense
DOE	Department of Energy
DTST	Defensive Technologies Study Team (Fletcher Committee)
GLCM	ground-launched cruise missile
HADS	high altitude defense system
HF laser	hydrogen fluoride laser
HOE	homing overlay experiment
HSD	hard site defense
ICBM	intercontinental ballistic missile
IR laser	infrared laser
MIRV	multiple independently targetable reentry vehicle
R&D	research and development
RDT&E	research, development, testing, and engineering
RV	reentry vehicle
SALT	Strategic Arms Limitation Talks
SAM	surface-to-air missile
SCC	Standing Consultative Commission
SDI	Strategic Defense Initiative
SLBM	submarine-launched ballistic missile
START	Strategic Arms Reduction Talks

SECTION I

Introduction

In his address to the nation on March 23, 1983, President Reagan announced "a decision which offers a new hope for our children in the 21st century. . . . " The vision was one of escape from the grim reliance on the threat of retaliation to deter aggression and prevent nuclear war. It was offered in the expressed conviction "that the human spirit must be capable of rising above dealing with other nations and human beings by threatening their existence." He asked the questions, "Wouldn't it be better to save lives than to avenge them? . . . What if free people could live secure in the knowledge that their security did not rest upon the threat of instant U.S. retaliation to deter a Soviet attack, that we could intercept and destroy strategic ballistic missiles before they reached our soil or that of our allies?" His answer was "I believe there is a way. . . . It is that we embark on a program to counter the awesome Soviet missile threat with measures that are defensive. . . . I call upon the scientific community in our country, those who gave us nuclear weapons, to turn their great talents now to the cause of mankind and world peace, to give us the means of rendering these nuclear weapons impotent and obsolete." The President concluded by characterizing his decision as one "which holds the promise of changing the course of human history."[1]

The vision expressed by the President appeals to powerful natural and moral sentiments. Indefinite reliance on the threat of retaliation by means of weapons of immense destructive power and conceivably apocalyptic effects is a forbidding prospect. Easing the balance of terror, and lessening and if possible removing the threat of nuclear war, have been preoccupations of responsible leaders since 1945. The impulse to look to our

[1] See the concluding section of President Reagan's speech, Appendix A.

1

weapons and armed forces to *defend us* rather than threaten others is a natural one—and has precedent in the history of ABM (anti-ballistic missile) development and negotiations over the past two decades.

Soviet preoccupation with defense is well known; Soviet interest in ABM systems will be described in Section II. In addition to the active Soviet ABM research and development program, and the existing deployment around Moscow, the most famous expression is the statement attributed by *Pravda* to A. N. Kosygin in London on February 9, 1967: "I think that a defensive system which prevents attack is not a cause of the arms race. . . . Perhaps an anti-missile system is more expensive than an offensive system; but its purpose is not to kill people but to save human lives."

President Nixon, in explaining his decision on March 14, 1969, to forego reluctantly a broad defense of the nation in favor of the limited Safeguard ABM system primarily to defend U.S. retaliatory forces, said in part:

> *Although every instinct motivates me to provide the American people with complete protection against a major nuclear attack* [emphasis added], it is not now within our power to do so. The heaviest defense system we considered, one designed to protect our major cities, still could not prevent a catastrophic level of U.S. fatalities from a deliberate all-out Soviet attack. And it might look to an opponent like the prelude to an offensive strategy threatening the Soviet deterrent.[2]

Thus serious pursuit of ABM is not a new idea in the strategic arms race. Acceptance in 1972 of the ABM Treaty[3] and of strictly limited deployments of ABM systems in the Soviet Union and the United States did not reflect any lack of awareness on either side of strategic defense and the arguments for it. Rather, it was a pragmatic conclusion. Whatever the abstract desirability of ABM defenses, in the early 1970s each of the superpowers, in sum, judged nationwide deployment of ABM to be *futile*, *destabilizing*, and *costly*.

- *Futile*: because in a competition between offensive missiles with nuclear warheads and defensive systems, the offense would win—especially against populations and urban areas.

- *Destabilizing*: because the arms race would be accelerated, as both sides developed and deployed not only competing ABM systems, but also offsetting systems to overpower, evade, or attack and disable the opposing ABM system. Further, each side would fear the purpose or the capability of the other's ABMs (especially against a weakened

---

[2] U.S. Arms Control and Disarmament Agency, *Documents on Disarmament, 1969* (Washington D.C.: USGPO, 1970), p. 103.
[3] The text of the ABM Treaty is included in Appendix D.

2

retaliatory strike), and in a crisis these fears could bring mounting pressures for striking first. What strategic theorists refer to as arms race instability and crisis instability could both result.

- *Costly*: because both ABM development and deployment, and the buildup, modernization, and diversification of offsetting offensive forces must be paid for. And the offensive countermeasures to maintain the reciprocal deterrent threat of intolerable retaliatory damage appeared not only capable of overwhelming the defense, but also easier and less costly.

More than a decade later, President Reagan has challenged the nation to reexamine these earlier judgments. Have the technological advances and strategic developments of the past decade, or those now in prospect, made it practical for us to realize his vision of a virtually leakproof defense which renders nuclear weapons impotent and obsolete? How would any potential change in technical and systems feasibility affect stability and costs?

Reexamination began in the Department of Defense (DOD), and has resulted in the Strategic Defense Initiative (SDI) program submitted to the Congress in early 1984. That program addresses not only the President's broad goal of *escaping* from reliance on deterrence, but also (and predominantly) an alternative or interim goal of *enhancing* deterrence. Dr. Richard DeLauer, Under Secretary of Defense for Research and Engineering, told the House Committee on Armed Services in submitting this program that DOD studies to date have

> concluded that advanced defensive technologies could offer the potential to enhance deterrence and help prevent nuclear war by reducing significantly the military utility of Soviet preemptive attacks and by undermining an aggressor's confidence of a successful attack against the United States or our allies.[4]

At present, he went on, uncertainties as to "the technical characteristics of defensive systems and the possible responses of the Soviet Union" make it impossible to decide which goal would be feasible and desirable to pursue. The FY 1985-89 program (projected to total $26 billion) is therefore a research effort to obtain the technical information and "experimental evidence" on which to base "an informed decision on whether and how to proceed. . . . "

Despite present uncertainties, the program is proposed, in DeLauer's words, on the premise that

[4] For a clear, brief, and informative summary of the program, see the *Statement on the President's Strategic Defense Initiative*, by the Hon. Richard D. DeLauer, Under Secretary of Defense for Research and Engineering, Appendix C.

we believe that an effective defense against ballistic missiles could have far-reaching implications for enhanced deterrence, greater stability, and improved opportunities for arms control. Our efforts do not seek to replace proven policies for maintaining the peace, but rather to strengthen their effectiveness in the face of a growing Soviet threat.

Other Administration spokesmen have argued further that a partially effective defense, should deterrence fail, would provide some protection to urban-industrial areas and thus limit damage and save lives.

The President's March 23 speech contained elements which foreshadowed this alternative goal of an "effective" but partial defense to enhance deterrence. He emphasized that

as we proceed, we must remain constant in preserving the nuclear deterrent and maintaining a solid capability for flexible response . . . we recognize that our allies rely upon our strategic offensive power to deter attacks against them. . . . We must and shall continue to honor our commitments.

With regard to control and reduction of nuclear arms, he reaffirmed his policy of *"negotiating from a position of strength* that can be assured only by modernizing our strategic forces . . . " [emphasis supplied].

Whether the SDI is directed at exploring a nearly leakproof defense *transcending* deterrence, or an effective but partial defense *enhancing* deterrence, the President's initiative has raised basic issues that go to the heart of the superpower strategic relationship and of approaches to the avoidance of nuclear war. It is the purpose of this study to contribute to assessment and debate, not only on technical feasibility and cost, but also on the strategic, political, and arms control implications of the program and its goals.

Since the Soviet Union is the other major participant both in the strategic relationship and in arms control, its posture on ABM is a major factor to be examined. How will the Soviets perceive the President's goal and the U.S. programs set in motion to move toward it? The initial Soviet reaction, voiced by General Secretary Andropov himself, was harsh and negative. What can we know or infer about Soviet views of the ABM Treaty, of continuing ABM-related research and development in the Soviet Union and the United States, about deterrence and the role of nuclear weapons? How might the Soviet Union react—in its weapons programs, arms control negotiations, and other aspects of U.S.-Soviet relations—to an ABM program initiated by the United States and advocated by our leaders, whatever its stated purpose? And, recognizing the role that U.S.-Soviet strategic relations play in the security calculations of our allies and other countries, how are these nations likely to calculate their own security interests and the impact of ABM programs and goals on international

4

stability and the prospects of nuclear war? We can address such questions now with varying degrees of confidence and uncertainty. Even where uncertainty prevails, we can identify important factors and interactions to be watched as research proceeds, as well as possible risks or opportunities.

The President has proposed no specific systems deployment and has stated that at least initially all activities will be consistent with the limitations of the ABM Treaty concluded in SALT I. We shall examine the problems that may arise in complying with the Treaty when the time comes for the "technology demonstration" tests that the DOD proposes to conduct.

The SDI program that has been defined is presented as a long-term R&D program leading to options from which a president may choose in the 1990s. Despite this long lead time, one very basic fact should be understood by all, citizens and officials alike. The new program differs significantly from the U.S. program to date, whose aim has been to offer a prudent "hedge" against technical breakthroughs, and to guard against Soviet technical advances and even unilateral ABM development. It is now directed toward a presidentially stated goal in accordance with a strategic concept at odds with the premises of current U.S. and Soviet strategic relations, and also of arms control negotiations, of which the ABM Treaty is the principal and most central result. The change may prove eventually to be salutary, the new direction sound; but just now it is unilateral change to which the Soviet Union will have to respond in accordance with its perception of what may be the intended or actual impact of U.S. actions on Soviet security. The Soviets are not likely to defer adjustments in their ABM and offensive strategic programs, or in their positions in the START negotiations, until the United States makes its formal deployment decisions five to ten years hence. They will not want to lag behind our ABM programs. And in the face of a presidential commitment to ABM which threatens their deterrent capability, they are unlikely to look sympathetically at U.S. START proposals for deep reductions in their most effective deterrent missiles and warheads. Thus the new SDI of the United States—whatever its eventual fate—is not a cost-free enterprise in strategic and arms control terms, any more than it is in economic ones.[5]

To reduce uncertainties in the future strategic relationship and to keep

[5] The MIRV (multiple independently targetable reentry vehicle) precedent is in the minds of many as we try to judge this new venture. MIRVs were originally designed to exploit U.S. technological capabilities to enhance, at a lesser cost, the effectiveness of U.S. deterrent retaliatory forces in the face of the initial Soviet deployment of defenses around Moscow and in anticipation of further system growth. But MIRVs were not abandoned when the ABM Treaty severely limited Soviet ABM and upgrading of air defenses. And as the Soviets in turn deployed MIRVs, especially on land-based ICBMs, they became a focus of strategic instability and U.S. concern.

our options open, we should be careful how we structure the SDI program and explain it to our allies and to the Soviet Union. Indeed, as will be shown below, the ABM Treaty calls for just such a dialogue between the two parties before any tests even of components of advanced new ABM technologies. Quite aside from Treaty provisions, it is in the interest of strategic stability and arms control prospects to explain fully and privately to the Soviet Union why we see the SDI as a possible way to reduce the risk of nuclear war and the pace of the arms race, not as a way to a U.S. strategic superiority to be used for our political ends against their legitimate interests.

Finally, we shall look directly at the most basic question raised by the President in his speech. What should we do, if we wish to escape as far as possible from the shadow of nuclear weapons and the fear of nuclear war? This question preoccupies many people today, in the United States and in other countries—proponents of arms control and detente, sincere advocates of peace and deterrence through military strength, the nuclear freeze movement in the United States and the peace movement in Europe, the Catholic bishops and other religious leaders, and many others. The President has proposed a solution dependent on future advances in weapons technology. Are there other avenues by which men and nations can escape the threat of nuclear war and the need to rely on nuclear deterrence with its threat of retaliation? The strict limitation of ABM, the ABM Treaty, and associated U.S.-Soviet arms control and political understandings have a broader significance in this context that is often forgotten. Beyond its function as a damper on the impetus to continuing competitive strategic force improvement and expansion, the ABM Treaty is a charter for the superpowers' recognition of the consequences of nuclear war, and their acceptance of the need for cooperative action, including arms control, if they are to live safely under the shadow of nuclear weapons and to make progress toward a world free of that shadow. Since the ABM Treaty is so central to the present strategic relationship and the fragile degree of stability that now obtains, we turn first to a review of the Treaty. What does it call for? How did the Soviets and the United States come to accept it? What is its contribution to mutual deterrence, prevention of nuclear war, and arms control?

The ABM Treaty and the U.S.-Soviet Strategic Relationship

The ABM Treaty

In his March 23 speech, President Reagan began his announcement of his new program by referring explicitly to the 1972 ABM Treaty: "Tonight, consistent with our obligations of the ABM Treaty . . . I'm taking an important first step." In testimony before the Senate Armed Services Committee that same day, though apparently without awareness of the President's imminent speech, Major General Grayson D. Tate, Jr., Ballistic Missile Defense Program Manager, listed "adherence to the ABM Treaty"[6] as one of the governing criteria of the R&D program he managed. What does the ABM Treaty require, and what is involved in acting in a way "consistent with the ABM Treaty," during any research and development program, and in any ABM deployment or related activity? We will identify current and prospective problems of interpretation and compliance.

Relevant Provisions of the ABM Treaty

The ABM Treaty is of indefinite duration. It is carefully crafted, and constitutes a systematic effort to design a treaty which can remain effective in the face of technological change whose exact nature could not at the time be foreseen.

Article I, paragraph 2, states what is prohibited and what is permitted, in general terms both as to purpose and as to effect:

[6] *Strategic and Theatre Nuclear Forces*, Hearings before the Committee on Armed Services: Department of Defense Authorization for Appropriations for Fiscal Year 1984 (March-May 1983), U.S. Senate, 98th Congress, First Session (Washington D.C.: USGPO, 1983), p. 2682.

2. Each Party undertakes not to deploy ABM systems for a defense of the territory of its country and not to provide a base for such a defense, and not to deploy ABM systems for defense of an individual region except as provided for in Article III of this Treaty.

Article III describes in detail the two permitted regional defense deployments, one centered on the national capital, the other containing ICBM fields. (The 1974 Protocol to the Treaty reduced to one the number of permitted regional deployments.) Article VII permits "subject to the provisions of this Treaty, modernization and replacement of ABM systems or their components . . . "; Article IV governs the number and locations of additional ABM components engaged in development or testing.

Article V specifies a number of types of ABM components, or modes of deployment, which are categorically prohibited; those in pararaph 1 are prohibited largely because their mobility means that they are inherently difficult to limit to regional defense.

1. Each party undertakes not to develop, test, or deploy ABM systems or components which are sea-based, air-based, space-based, or mobile land-based.

The inconsistency between Article V.1 and the ABM systems envisaged in the President's speech is self-evident. For the initial research and development stage of the broadened U.S. ABM program, the first issue in assuring adherence to the ABM Treaty relates to what should be understood by the terms "development" and "testing," which will be discussed further. It should be noted that similar questions arise already regarding the existing ballistic missile defense program described in Major General Tate's 1983 testimony. The High Altitude Defense System (HADS) therein described includes a Homing Overlay Experiment (HOE) and an Airborne Optical Adjunct (AOA) described in these terms:

The primary objective of the HOE effort is flight test demonstrations of high altitude optical homing and nonnuclear kill. The first HOE flight occurred last February and [deleted] intercept of a reentry vehicle using a nonnuclear kill device.

The Airborne Optical Adjunct (AOA) . . . will consist of an aircraft-based optical sensor system [deleted] BMD system concepts. Use of the AOA [deleted] will greatly extend the battle space, present an attacker the problem of having to counter dual phenomenology sensors (optics and radar). . . .[7]

These activities appear inconsistent with the Treaty limits on air- or space-based ABM component development and testing. They illustrate the problems of Treaty compliance to be encountered as space-based

[7] Ibid., p. 2683.

8

elements (sensors and kill devices particularly) advance in development in the United States or the Soviet Union. Similarly, development of a mobile ABM radar (the Sentry) in the Hard Site Defense (HSD) program could raise compliance questions as a "mobile land-based" component.

To assist in coping with these ambiguities, some identifiable in 1972 and some which could be foreseen only vaguely, Article VI and Agreed Statement D were formulated. Article II defines an ABM system as "a system to counter *strategic* ballistic missiles or their elements in flight trajectory . . . " [emphasis supplied]. There are non-strategic missile systems as well as aircraft against which launchers, interceptors, and radars can be used. These in turn might have, or be given, a significant capability against strategic ballistic missiles. Article VI specifies that the *capability* of such systems to serve in an ABM capacity is to be limited, and that testing of such components, regardless of their primary purpose, in an ABM mode is banned:

> To enhance assurance of the effectiveness of the limitations on ABM systems and their components provided by the Treaty, each Party undertakes:
>
> (a) not to give missiles, launchers, or radars, other than ABM interceptor missiles, ABM launchers, or ABM radars, capabilities to counter strategic ballistic missiles or their elements in flight trajectory, and not to test them in an ABM mode; . . .

The U.S. pushed vigorously for this provision during the negotiations, both to clarify the application of the Treaty, and to facilitate verification.

In a Unilateral Statement on April 7, 1972, neither challenged nor endorsed by the Soviet delegation, the U.S. delegation listed a number of examples of what would be considered "tested in an ABM mode." Since then the U.S. has been vigilant in monitoring and challenging Soviet activities, mainly in air defense programs, which might be inconsistent with this provision. Currently the United States has programs underway to determine whether the U.S. Hawk and Patriot surface-to-air missile systems for air defense could be given anti-tactical missile capabilities. If such developments go ahead (and the Soviets have similar ones), the question of inherent ABM capability and consistency with Article VI will arise.

Agreed Statement D attempts to lay a basis for dealing with unforeseeable ways in which the onward march of technology might change the means used for ABM defense (which Article II describes as currently consisting of ABM interceptor missiles, ABM launchers, and ABM radars with defined characteristics). It reads as follows:

> In order to insure fulfillment of the obligation not to deploy ABM systems and their components except as provided in Article III of the Treaty, the Parties

9

agree that in the event ABM systems based on other physical principles and including components capable of substituting for ABM interceptor missiles, ABM launchers, or ABM radars are created in the future, specific limitations on such systems and their components would be subject to discussion in accordance with Article XIII and agreement in accordance with Article XIV of the Treaty.

Since the contingency referred to has not yet arisen—though it is imminent—the precise meaning of the Statement has not been finally determined, and its application has not been established. The literal meaning has been argued to be that such "exotic" ABM systems or components could only be developed, tested, or deployed *after* amendment of the Treaty (Article XIV).

Taken in conjunction with Article V, with its categorical prohibitions, there seems to be no alternative interpretation in the case of sea-, air-, space-, and mobile land-based systems. Thus the effect of the Agreed Statement is to make clear that "exotic" systems or technologies are not exempt from the limitations of the Treaty although they are not mentioned specifically, but that they are not ruled out permanently *provided* the parties amend the Treaty first to permit them, within agreed limitations. Such possibilities might be identified and explored in the Standing Consultative Commission (SCC) (Article XIII), though that would not be the exclusive channel of course. If the United States pursues a space-based ABM system development and testing program, the Soviet Union has a clear option to raise questions in the SCC regarding its intent and character. The United States has an obligation under Article XIII.b "to provide on a voluntary basis" such information as will answer these questions if the Soviet Union should raise them.

One broad area of ambiguity in applying the Treaty is the scope of the term "development," as used in the Treaty, and as applied to R&D programs of the two parties. Ambassador Gerard Smith provided the Nixon Administration's interpretation of the term on June 18, 1972, in his testimony before the Senate Armed Services Committee during Senate consideration of the SALT I agreements:

> Article V of the ABM Treaty and an Agreed Interpretive Statement (E) obligate the U.S. and U.S.S.R. "not to develop, test, or deploy" mobile ABM systems, rapid reload devices, or ABM interceptor missiles for delivery of more than one independently guided warhead.
>
> The SALT negotiating history clearly supports the following interpretation. The obligation not to develop such systems, devices or warheads would be applicable only to the stage of development which follows laboratory development and testing. The prohibitions on development contained in the ABM Treaty would start at that part of the development process where field testing is initiated on

either a prototype or breadboard model. It was understood by both sides that the prohibition on "development" applies to activities involved after a component moves from the laboratory development and testing stage to the field testing stage, wherever performed. The fact that early stages of the development process, such as laboratory testing, would pose problems for verification by national technical means is an important consideration in reaching this definition. Exchanges with the Soviet Delegation made clear that this definition is also the Soviet interpretation of the term "development."

Consequently, there is adequate basis for the interpretation that development as used in Article V of the ABM Treaty and as applied to the budget categories in the DOD RDT&E program places no constraints on research and on those aspects of exploratory and advanced development which precede field testing. Engineering development would clearly be prohibited.[8]

This statement is helpful, but one can foresee sharp disagreements between the parties, as each represents its own R&D activities as falling within the permitted early stages of the development process, but argues that detectable or suspected activities of the other raise serious questions of compliance.

One specific instance of likely ambiguity and dispute brings two other treaties into play. One possible novel technology for ABM kill involves a high energy laser driven by a nuclear explosion in space. Deployment in orbit of such a device would clearly be contrary to Article IV of the Outer Space Treaty of 1967:

States Parties to the Treaty undertake not to place in orbit around the Earth any objects carrying nuclear weapons or any other kinds of weapons of mass destruction, install such weapons on celestial bodies, or station such weapons in outer space in any other manner. . . .[9]

Testing in space or the atmosphere would also be banned by the Limited Nuclear Test Ban Treaty of 1963.

One other provision of the ABM Treaty should be noted. It is Article IX:

[8] *Military Implications of the Treaty on the Limitations of Anti-Ballistic Missile Systems and the Interim Agreement on Limitation of Strategic Offensive Arms,* Hearing before the Committee on Armed Services (June-July 1972), U.S. Senate, 92nd Congress, Second Session (Washington D.C.: USGPO, 1972), p. 377. This statement, and particularly its final sentence, provide illuminating background for an observation of the Scowcroft Commission in its final report to the President on March 21, 1984: "[But] the strategic implications of ballistic missile defense and the criticality of the ABM Treaty to further arms control agreements dictate extreme caution in proceeding to engineering development in this sensitive area." See the *Report of the President's Commission on Strategic Forces,* March 21, 1984, p. 8.

[9] Text of the "Treaty on Principles Governing the Activities of States in the Exploration and Use of Outer Space, Including the Moon and Other Celestial Bodies," U.S. Arms Control and Disarmament Agency, *Arms Control and Disarmament Agreements: Texts and Histories of Negotiations* (Washington D.C.: USGPO, 1980), p. 51.

11

To assure the viability and effectiveness of this Treaty, each Party undertakes not to transfer to other States, and not to deploy outside its national territory, ABM systems or their components limited by this Treaty.

A principal attraction of the newly proposed ABM systems is the possibility of engaging attacking strategic ballistic missiles in boost phase, before reentry vehicles have separated into individual targets, and early enough to permit layered subsequent attacks on surviving reentry vehicles. Such a scenario places very stringent time limits—a few minutes only—on detecting, identifying and tracking, and attacking the hostile missiles. To facilitate timely action, and perhaps avoid the vulnerability of components deployed in advance in space, consideration has been given to forward deployment of key components—especially the lasers which might be mounted on missiles and launched on receipt of notification of enemy attack (i.e., "pop up"), executing their kill mission with less interference from curvature of the earth. Article IX, however, would clearly ban deployment outside the United States (e.g., in the United Kingdom, Canada, or outside of U.S. territorial waters).

So far, specific limitations on ABM systems set forth in the ABM Treaty and other agreements have been discussed, along with examples of compliance issues. No less relevant is the basic rationale of the ABM Treaty, as set forth in the Preamble:

> The United States of America and the Union of Soviet Socialist Republics, hereinafter referred to as the Parties,
>
> Proceeding from the premise that nuclear war would have devastating consequences for all mankind,
>
> Considering that effective measures to limit anti-ballistic missile systems would be a substantial factor in curbing the race in strategic offensive arms and would lead to a decrease in the risk of outbreak of war involving nuclear weapons,
>
> Proceeding from the premise that the limitation of anti-ballistic missile systems, as well as certain agreed measures with respect to the limitation of strategic offensive arms, would contribute to the creation of more favorable conditions for further negotiations on limiting strategic arms, . . .

The President's speech takes direct issue with this rationale, though the program initially being undertaken is more conditionally framed (to examine whether there are technologies that might emerge in the distant future and that hold some promise of defense against missile attack). Even as a conditional program—as distinct from the previous U.S. research program justified as a prudent hedge against technical surprise or breakout[10]—the purpose and rationale of the Treaty are brought unilat-

[10] Breakout means the resumption of ABM deployment after renunciation of, or withdrawal from, the Treaty.

erally and unequivocally into question. An obligation to explain what the United States is now undertaking, and discuss it in the SCC, is implicit in Article XIII. Quite aside from the question of legal obligation, such action could be prudent to avoid suspicions and dangerous reactions, particularly if we attach importance to the ABM Treaty for the present until some better approach to strategic stability and arms reduction is jointly accepted by both nations. Among other benefits, suspicions of U.S. preparations for breakout from the Treaty (a frequently expressed U.S. concern about Soviet ABM R&D activities) might be avoided or allayed. This matter will be discussed further in Section IV.

Soviet Perspectives on the ABM Treaty

President Reagan's call for a new ABM project raises basic questions going beyond the issue of technical prospects for new ABM systems. How will the effort to develop such systems affect United States security, the risk of nuclear war, and prospects for arms control? These questions cannot be answered without taking account of possible Soviet responses to United States policy.

Soviet Policy and the ABM Treaty

Soviet work on ABM systems began in the late 1940s or early 1950s, in parallel with the development of offensive missiles. This effort was a natural outgrowth of the intensive program to build air defenses. When Soviet military doctrine and strategy were reassessed in the late 1950s and early 1960s, ABM systems were assigned a very important role.

Marshal V. D. Sokolovskii's *Military Strategy* (1962), the most important study of strategy published during that period, declared that "one of the cardinal problems for Soviet military strategy is the reliable defense of the rear from nuclear strikes." Sokolovskii stated that ABM defenses, along with other measures, "ought to lower as much as possible the losses from the enemy's nuclear strikes, to preserve the viability of the country's rear and the combat capability of the Armed Forces." The National Air Defense Forces (which have responsibility for anti-missile systems) would have the "main role in protecting the country's territory from these [nuclear] strikes, in repulsing the enemy's nuclear attack."[11]

Sokolovskii acknowledged that "in contemporary conditions the means and methods of nuclear attack unquestionably prevail over the means and methods of defense against them."[12] But claims made by Nikita Khrush-

[11] Marshal V. D. Sokolovskii, *Voyennaya Strategiya* [Military strategy] (Moscow: Voyenizdat, 1962), pp. 231, 271.
[12] Ibid., p. 231.

chev and other officials in the early 1960s suggested that the Soviet Union had found a way of carrying out the mission of strategic defense. In 1961 Marshal R. Ya. Malinovskii, the Minister of Defense, stated that "the problem of destroying enemy missiles in flight has been successfully resolved."[13] In 1962 Khrushchev asserted that the Soviet Union had developed an ABM missile that could "hit a fly in space."[14] The Soviet Union started to deploy an ABM system around Leningrad in the early 1960s, but this was soon abandoned. Later in the decade work began on an ABM system around Moscow, and this remains the most substantial deployment to date.

Soviet ABM policy was rooted in both military strategy and political sentiment. ABM systems were designed, as Sokolovskii said, to limit the damage that an enemy nuclear strike would cause, and to enable the state and the Armed Forces to continue to function in time of war. It was also hoped that they would make it possible for the Soviet Union to base its security on something other than the balance of terror. Major-General N. Talenskii, a leading military theorist, wrote in 1964 that "the creation of an effective antimissile system enables the state to make its own defenses dependent chiefly on its own possibilities, and not only on mutual deterrence, that is, on the goodwill of the other side."[15]

But in the late 1960s Soviet attitudes began to change. In 1967 and 1968, as the Soviet leaders were preparing for SALT, various military leaders offered different evaluations of the effectiveness of ABM systems. The Commander-in-Chief of the National Air Defense Forces, Army General P. F. Batitskii, claimed that Soviet defenses could "reliably protect the territory of the country against ballistic missile attack."[16] But the Commander-in-Chief of the Strategic Missile Forces, Marshal N. I. Krylov, stated that offensive missiles had characteristics that in practice guaranteed the "invulnerability of ballistic missiles in flight, especially when employed in mass."[17] In 1967 and 1968 work on the ABM system around Moscow slowed down, and only four of the eight complexes were completed. The Soviet authorities evidently had little confidence in its effectiveness.[18]

[13] *Pravda*, October 25, 1961.
[14] Theodore Shabad, "Khrushchev Says Missile Can 'Hit a Fly' in Space," *New York Times*, July 17, 1962, p. 1.
[15] Maj. Gen. N. Talenskii, "Anti-Missile Systems and Disarmament," *International Affairs*, 1964, no. 10, p. 18.
[16] Interview, Radio Moscow, February 20, 1967. Quoted by Raymond L. Garthoff, "BMD and East-West Relations," Ashton B. Carter and David N. Schwartz, eds., *Ballistic Missile Defense* (Washington, D.C.: The Brookings Institution, 1984), pp. 295-96.
[17] Marshal N. I. Krylov, "Raketnye voiska strategicheskogo naznacheniya" [Strategic rocket forces], *Voyenno-istoricheskii zhurnal*, 1967, no. 7, p. 20.
[18] For an excellent analysis of Soviet ABM programs see Sayre Stevens, "The Soviet BMD Program," Carter and Schwartz, eds., op. cit., pp. 182-220.

Alongside the growing doubts about the effectiveness of ABM systems came an increasing confidence in the deterrent power of the Soviet Union's offensive strategic forces. By the end of the 1960s the Soviet Union was approaching strategic parity with the United States. In 1973 Major General M. Cherednichenko, one of Marshal Sokolovskii's closest collaborators, wrote in the classified General Staff journal *Military Thought* that the Soviet Union had now

> acquired the capability of delivering a devastating nuclear response to an aggressor in any and all circumstances, even under conditions of a sneak nuclear attack, and of inflicting on the aggressor a critical level of damage. An unusual situation developed: an aggressor who would initiate a nuclear war would irrevocably be subjected to a devastating return nuclear strike by the other side. It proved unrealistic for an aggressor to count on victory in such a war, in view of the enormous risk for the aggressor's own continued existence.[19]

The Soviet Union acknowledged at SALT that each side was vulnerable to a devastating retaliatory strike if it attacked first. The opening Soviet statement (as summarized by Gerard Smith, the chief American negotiator) declared that

> mountains of weapons were growing, yet security was not improving but diminishing as a result. A situation of mutual deterrence existed. Even in the event that one of the sides was the first to be subjected to attack, it would undoubtedly retain the ability to inflict a retaliatory blow of destructive force. It would be tantamount to suicide for the ones who decided to start war.[20]

This did not mean, in Soviet eyes, that nuclear war was impossible. The Soviet Union showed concern at SALT about the danger of war by miscalculation, and about the possibility that a third nuclear state might provoke a world war. The Soviet Union and the United States agreed upon various measures to reduce the danger of accidental war. The Soviet Union sought, but did not obtain, cooperation from the United States in dealing with the nuclear threat from China, although the Agreement on the Prevention of Nuclear War (1973) may have given it something of what it wanted.

Soviet policy at SALT was based on the recognition that the existing nuclear balance could be upset by the deployment of either offensive or defensive systems. Major-General Zemskov wrote in *Military Thought* in May 1969 that the nuclear balance of power could be disrupted either by a sharp increase in one side's offensive forces, or by "the creation by one of the sides of highly effective means of protection from a nuclear attack of the enemy in conditions when the other side lags considerably in

[19] Maj. Gen. M. Cherednichenko, "Military Strategy and Military Technology," *Voyennaya Mysl*, 1973, no. 4, FPD 0043, November 12, 1973, p. 53.
[20] Gerard Smith, *Doubletalk, The Story of SALT I* (New York: Doubleday, 1980), p. 83.

resolution of these missions."[21] If the United States tilted the balance in its favor, he wrote, the danger of nuclear war would grow.

Given this view of the strategic balance, it seems likely that the fear of an unconstrained race in ABM systems played some part in convincing the Soviet leaders of the desirability of the ABM Treaty. At one point during the negotiations the Soviet Union proposed that ABM systems be considered separately, thus suggesting particular concern about a race in defensive systems. But this was not the only factor in the decision to sign the Treaty. The Soviet leaders were aware that the deployment of ABM systems would stimulate the further development of offensive forces. During the exploratory moves before SALT, the Soviet Union had asked that defensive and offensive systems be considered together. The Preamble to the ABM Treaty notes that "effective measures to limit anti-ballistic missile systems would be a substantial factor in curbing the race in strategic offensive arms." Marshal A. A. Grechko, the Defense Minister, claimed in September 1972 that the Treaty prevented "the development of a competition between offensive and defensive rocket-nuclear weapons."[22]

Although the Soviet discussion of ABM systems was very different from the contemporary American debate, some of the arguments advanced against ABM systems were the same: ABM systems would not be effective against offensive missiles; ABM deployment would spur the other side into increasing its offensive forces; and ABM deployment could upset the nuclear balance, and this might increase the danger of war if the balance were tilted in the American favor.

Because the Soviet press treated these issues very warily, the Soviet debate of the late 1960s is difficult to reconstruct. One of the most outspoken documents to come to us is an interview that Andrei Sakharov gave to the Soviet journalist Ernst Henry in 1967. Sakharov was still working in the military sector, and he and Henry intended to use this interview as the basis for an article to be published in the Soviet press, but this was apparently banned by the Party Central Committee. Part of the interview reads as follows:

Sakharov: As everyone knows, the United States and the Soviet Union possess enormous stockpiles of strategic missiles with thermonuclear warheads. The two countries are, speaking figuratively, armed with nuclear "swords." The construction of an antimissile defense system would mean adding a "shield" to the "sword." I think that such an expansion of nuclear missile armament would be very dangerous.

Henry: Why?

[21] Maj. Gen. V. M. Zemskov, "Wars of the Modern Era," *Voyennaya Mysl*, 1969, no. 5, FPD 0117/69, p. 60.
[22] *Pravda*, September 30, 1972.

16

Sakharov: This is why. Under the present political and technological conditions, a "shield" could create the illusion of invulnerability. For the "hawks" and "madmen," a shield would increase the lure of nuclear blackmail. It would strengthen their attraction to the idea of a "preventive" thermonuclear strike.[23]

The ABM Treaty removed, for the time being at least, the illusion that such a "shield" could be created: the Soviet Union and the United States were now clearly vulnerable to retaliatory strikes by the other, no matter who struck first.

This recognition of mutual vulnerability has remained central to the Soviet conception of the Soviet-American strategic relationship. Brezhnev, for example, told the 26th Party Congress in 1981 that "the military and strategic equilibrium prevailing between the USSR and the USA . . . is objectively a safeguard of world peace. We have not sought, and do not now seek, military superiority over the other side." He also declared that "to try to outstrip each other in the arms race or to expect to win a nuclear war is dangerous madness."[24] In September 1983, Marshal N.V. Ogarkov, the Chief of the General Staff, wrote that

> with the modern development and dispersion of nuclear arms in the world, the defending side will always retain such a quantity of nuclear means as will be capable of inflicting "unacceptable damage," as the former Defense Secretary of the USA, R. McNamara, characterized it in his time, on the aggressor in a retaliatory strike.[25]

And in words that echo the opening Soviet statement at SALT in November 1969, he added that "in contemporary conditions only suicides can wager on a first nuclear strike."

The Soviet leaders appear to recognize this mutual vulnerability to devastating retaliatory strikes as an objective condition, but they have not embraced it with enthusiasm. They have shown concern about the possibility of war by accident or miscalculation. They have also thought it prudent to prepare for nuclear war, in case it should occur. According to the *Military Encyclopedic Dictionary*, published in 1983 and edited by Marshal Ogarkov,

> in accordance with Soviet military doctrine, which has a profoundly defensive character, the main task of Soviet military strategy is to develop the means of repulsing the aggressor's attack and then defeating him utterly by means of conducting decisive operations.[26]

[23] Andrei Sakharov and Ernst Henry, "Scientists and Nuclear War," Stephen F. Cohen, ed., *An End to Silence* (New York: W. W. Norton & Co., 1982), p. 230.

[24] *Pravda*, February 24, 1981.

[25] *Krasnaya Zvezda*, September 23, 1983.

[26] Marshal N. V. Ogarkov, ed., *Voyennyi Entsiklopedicheskii Slovar'* [Military encyclopedic dictionary] (Moscow: Voyenizdat, 1983), p. 712.

Even within the confines of mutual vulnerability, Soviet military strategy still focuses on how to wage a nuclear war and defeat the enemy, if such a war should occur.

The Soviet leaders apparently accept that mutual vulnerability to devastating retaliatory strikes is an objective condition, for the time being at least, but their preparation for war arouses fears that they either do not recognize the reality of this condition, or are trying to escape from it. There is a tension between these two elements of Soviet thinking (as there is between deterrence and war-fighting in American thinking about nuclear war). Both elements have to be recognized if Soviet policy on ABM systems is to be understood.

Soviet ABM Policy Since 1972

In November 1973, the Commander-in-Chief of the National Air Defense Forces, Marshal P. F. Batitskii, wrote in *Military Thought* that "within the framework of the agreements limiting ABM defense, such defenses will in all probability change only qualitatively, and will remain limited in capability, able only to cover the capitals of the countries against prospective means of ballistic missile attack."[27] Since 1972 the Soviet Union has maintained a steady R&D effort in ABM technologies. This effort has five main elements.

First, the Soviet Union has been upgrading the Moscow ABM system, which had become fully operational in 1970 or 1971. Although it covered a very large footprint, this system, with only sixty-four Galosh exoatmospheric interceptor missiles, would have been almost wholly useless against a determined nuclear attack.

In 1980 the Soviet Union began to replace the Galosh missiles with SH-04 and SH-08 nuclear-armed interceptors. The SH-04 is an exoatmospheric missile, like Galosh, and the SH-08 is a hypersonic endoatmospheric missile, like the American Sprint. When only exoatmospheric missiles were available, a decision to launch would have had to been taken before the incoming reentry vehicles entered the atmosphere. Now the system can use atmospheric sorting to discriminate between real reentry vehicles and decoys. New phased-array radars (the Pushkino radar) are being built to perform the engagement function.[28]

These measures will make the Moscow system more effective against very limited or accidental attacks. But the system's capability should not be exaggerated. The radars are vulnerable to attack, and without them the

[27] Marshal P. F. Batitskii, "The National Air Defense Troops," *Voyennaya Mysl*, 1973, no. 11, FPD 0049, August 27, 1974, p. 36.
[28] See Clarence A. Robinson, Jr., "Soviets Accelerate Missile Defense Efforts," *Aviation Week and Space Technology (AWST)*, January 16, 1984, pp. 14-16.

system would be crippled. The number of interceptor missiles that the Soviet Union can deploy is limited to 100 by the ABM Treaty. Moreover, the reentry vehicles on the U.S. offensive missiles have increased greatly in number (from under 2,000 to over 7,000) and in sophistication since 1972. The upgrading of the Moscow system does not mark a significant shift in the Soviet-American strategic balance. It was long expected, and has not caused great concern in the United States.

Second, greater concern has been caused by the possibility that the SH-04 and SH-08 missiles might form part of a system (designated the ABM-X-3 defense system by the United States) that could be deployed rapidly to create a nationwide defense. New tracking and missile guidance radars have reportedly been developed to go with the interceptor missiles. These radars are designed modularly (which is now standard production practice in the United States as well) and are said to be suitable for fairly rapid deployment. With its large radar and missile industries the Soviet Union could produce the components of the ABM-X-3 system on an extensive scale. A recent report by the CIA has raised the specter of a Soviet breakout from the ABM Treaty. In the words of one United States official, "the U.S. could be witnessing a Soviet move to place itself in a position to abrogate the Antiballistic Missile Treaty and rapidly deploy a system to defend key areas such as intercontinental ballistic missile fields."[29]

There seems to be, however, no firm evidence that this is what the Soviet Union is doing. Even with modularly designed radars it would take years rather than months to deploy the new system on a significant scale. Such a system would not be leakproof and could be overwhelmed. Besides, the radars would be vulnerable to attack. If the Soviet Union attempted a breakout, the United States would have time to respond by improving the penetration of offensive forces. The Soviet Union would have to expect that the United States would respond in this way, and that it might even be provoked into deploying an ABM system of its own.

Third, the Soviet Union is constructing a radar at the village of Abalakova, near Krasnoyarsk. United States intelligence analysts believe that this is similar to the early warning radars at Pechora, Komsomol'sk-na-Amure, and Kiev. The Krasnoyarsk radar appears to be oriented outwards, toward the northeast, and could detect Trident missiles launched from the Bering Sea or the Gulf of Alaska. The Reagan Administration claims that this radar "almost certainly" violates Article VI.b of the ABM Treaty, which limits the deployment of ballistic missile early warning radars to locations along the borders of the two countries and requires

[29] The CIA report is discussed in ibid.

that they be oriented outwards. The Soviet Union has said that it is designed for space tracking and thus consistent with the ABM Treaty.[30]

Some anxiety has been expressed in the United States that if the Krasnoyarsk radar were linked with the Pechora radar, it would permit triangulation and a more accurate attack assessment than is possible from a single radar. Also, the proximity of the new radar to three of the six SS-18 ICBM fields has aroused concern on the grounds that it could be used for ABM battle management if interceptor missiles were deployed. But neither of these seems to be a plausible explanation for the deployment of the radar. First, if the Soviet Union wanted to improve its ability to assess an attack, it could have built another radar on the north coast, within the terms of the Treaty. Second, the Krasnoyarsk radar seems to be too far from the SS-18 fields to be designed for battle management.

The purpose of the Krasnoyarsk radar, which has not yet begun to radiate, remains unclear. It may in fact be an early warning radar, for it appears to fill a gap in the Soviet early warning system. Some reports suggest that it has been built where it is because the permafrost makes construction nearer the northeast coast very difficult. But this would seem to be a very weak excuse for violating the ABM Treaty. The military significance of this radar is negligible while it stands in isolation from interceptor missiles, and it would be vulnerable to destruction or blackout in a nuclear attack. But it does raise a serious issue of Treaty compliance.

Fourth, the issue of SAM upgrade caused difficulties in the SALT I negotiations. It has become even trickier since then. Soviet air defenses have responded to the challenge posed by improved U.S. aerodynamic systems, including cruise missiles, and the innovations that have been made to deal with smaller radar cross sections and shorter reaction times have raised the capability of SAMs against ballistic missile reentry vehicles.

The problem is most dramatically illustrated by the development of the mobile SA-12, which is reported to have been tested not only against aerodynamic systems, but also against ballistic missile reentry vehicles.[31] These tests would violate the ABM Treaty if those reentry vehicles were similar to the RVs on ICBMs or SLBMs. The SA-12 may have been designed for use against tactical or theatre ballistic missiles, and it may also have some capability against SLBM reentry vehicles. This system suggests that it may be necessary to modify the Treaty to cope with the growing ambiguity created by advances in technology.

---

[30] *The President's Report to the Congress on Soviet Noncompliance with Arms Control Agreements*, mimeo (Washington D.C.: The White House, Office of the Press Secretary, January 23, 1984), pp. 3-4; see also Robinson, loc. cit.; and Philip J. Klass, "U.S. Scrutinizing New Soviet Radar," *AWST*, August 22, 1983, pp. 19-20.

[31] Stevens, loc. cit., pp. 214-16; Robinson, loc. cit.

Fifth, the Soviet Union has been doing research into the use of directed energy for ABM purposes. Most estimates of the quality of Soviet research in this area put it on a level with that in the United States.[32] An installation at Saryshagan, the chief center for ABM systems development and testing, has drawn the attention of the United States intelligence community, some members of which have argued that it is an early prototype of a directed-energy ABM system; but there is no unanimity on this point.[33] It would be surprising if the Soviet Union were not doing research on directed energy ABM systems, at least as a hedge against the possibility of a technological breakthrough. But the Soviet Union would face the same uncertainties and problems as the United States in designing an ABM system, and therefore the arguments advanced in Section III would apply in the Soviet case as well.

The Soviet Union, although it equals the United States in directed energy research, lags in other technologies that are crucial for ABM systems. According to the U.S. Department of Defense, the United States has a lead in computers, optics, automated control, electro-optical sensors, propulsion, radar, software, telecommunications, and guidance systems.[34] The only area in which the Soviet Union is said to enjoy a substantial lead is in large rockets that could lift heavy loads into space.[35] The level of Soviet technology suggests that if the Soviet Union tried to break out of the ABM Treaty by deploying an advanced ABM system, it could not develop an effective system so rapidly as to deprive the United States of its ability to deliver a massive retaliatory strike.

This brief survey of Soviet ABM R&D and deployment activities points to several conclusions. First, although the Soviet Union may have violated some provisions of the ABM Treaty (and that is not proven), it has not broken out of the Treaty, in the sense of deploying an extensive ABM system. Second, the Soviet Union could not break out so rapidly as to endanger the deterrent power of U.S. offensive forces. Third, some Soviet ABM activities have pressed against the provisions of the Treaty. The firing of two SH-08 interceptor missiles from the same silo within two hours may make it necessary to clarify what Article V of the Treaty means when it speaks of the undertaking "not to develop, test, or deploy auto-

[32] For example, in 1982 the DOD estimated that the Soviet Union and the United States were equal in the directed energy basic technology area. See *The FY 1983 Department of Defense Program for Research, Development and Acquisition*, statement by the Hon. Richard D. DeLauer, Under Secretary of Defense for Research and Engineering, to the 97th Congress (Washington D.C.: U.S. Department of Defense, 1982), p. II-21.

[33] "Soviets Build Directed-Energy Weapon," *AWST*, July 28, 1980, p. 47.

[34] Statement by DeLauer, loc. cit. See also, R. Jeffrey Smith, "The Search for a Nuclear Sanctuary (I)," *Science*, July 1, 1983, p. 32.

[35] Charles Mohr, "Pentagon Supports Advanced Defense Despite Flaws," *New York Times*, March 9, 1984, p. 8.

matic or semi-automatic or other similar systems for rapid reload of ABM launchers." Fourth, although the Krasnoyarsk radar may violate Article VI.b of the Treaty (and that is not yet proven) its military significance would be negligible. Such a violation would have considerable political significance, however, because it would show the Soviet Union's insensitivity to its Treaty obligations. Fifth, continuing Soviet SAM development against tactical and intermediate-range missiles and cruise missiles, as well as aircraft, has complicated the problem of drawing the line between "ABM capabilities" and permitted SAM systems.

The Soviet ABM effort since 1972 has been steady and unfrenzied. It can be interpreted as an attempt to develop defenses in those areas not covered by the Treaty in order to cope with new offensive threats—cruise missiles and Pershing IIs, for example. It can be viewed as a hedge against American deployment of an ABM system—a hedge that may look very sensible by the end of the decade. It may also be aimed at exploring new technologies which may one day permit a radically new balance between the offense and the defense. Which pattern prevails is more crucial than the individual programs. But the available evidence, while it points to a reluctance to embrace with enthusiasm the relationship of mutual deterrence, does not justify claims that the Soviet Union has broken out of the ABM Treaty, or is preparing to do so in the near future. The arguments advanced against ABM systems in the Soviet discussion of the late 1960s— worries about the effectiveness of ABM, fear of a technological race in offensive and defensive systems, concern about the danger of war—still seem to have force today from the Soviet perspective.

There is considerable uncertainty about Soviet ABM activities and about the intentions that lie behind them. The Soviet ABM effort needs to be monitored very carefully, and questioned as appropriate in the SCC, to ensure that the Soviet Union does comply with the Treaty. U.S. research should be continued to guard against the possibility of a Soviet breakout.

The Soviet Reaction to President Reagan's Speech

The Soviet reaction to Reagan's speech was uncompromisingly hostile. The defensive purpose that Reagan claimed to be his goal was dismissed as camouflage for a more sinister offensive aim. In a statement issued on March 27, 1983, Yuri Andropov said that the defensive measures Reagan spoke of would seem defensive only to "someone not conversant with these matters."[36]

The United States, said Andropov, would continue to develop its strategic offensive forces and

[36] *Pravda*, March 27, 1983. See excerpts from Andropov's statement, Appendix B.

22

under these conditions the intention to secure itself the possibility of destroying with the help of ABM defenses the corresponding strategic systems of the other side, that is of rendering it incapable of dealing a retaliatory strike, is a bid to disarm the Soviet Union in the face of the United States nuclear threat.

This is certainly the kind of reaction one would expect from the United States if a Soviet leader proclaimed the intention of developing effective defenses against ballistic missiles. Secretary of Defense Weinberger has said, "I can't imagine a more destabilizing factor for the world than if the Soviets should acquire a thoroughly reliable defense against these missiles before we do."[37] There is no reason why Soviet leaders should feel differently about an American ABM system.

In 1982 both President L. I. Brezhnev and Defense Minister D. F. Ustinov had claimed that the Reagan Administration was pursuing military superiority with the aim of destroying socialism as a socioeconomic system.[38] The Soviet leaders have portrayed the United States' military programs—the MX ICBM, the Trident D-5 SLBM, the Pershing II, and the cruise missile programs—as part of a concerted effort to achieve strategic superiority. The Soviet leaders apparently feared that even if these programs did not enable the United States to escape from the threat of a retaliatory strike, they might give it a strategic advantage. Defense Minister Ustinov stated in July 1982 that

> the idea of military superiority has become really an obsession. It determines the content of all the actions of the American government, and the demands of the USA on its allies. Superiority is understood as synonymous with the attainment of a capability to strike a blow at the Soviet Union when and where Washington considers it expedient, calculating on the fact that the retaliatory blow at the USA will become less powerful than in other conditions.[39]

In this context it is not surprising that the immediate Soviet reaction was to view the President's speech with intense suspicion, and to present it as further evidence of the American drive for strategic superiority.

Besides portraying Reagan's strategic defense initiative as part of a drive to achieve superiority, Andropov argued that the attempt to build an ABM system would intensify the arms race. At SALT I, he said, the Soviet Union and the United States "agreed that there is an inseverable interconnection between strategic offensive and defensive weapons." "Only mutual restraint in the field of ABM defenses" would make progress possible in limiting and reducing offensive weapons. Now, said Andropov, "the United

[37] Gerald F. Seib, "Officials Say Reagan is Ready to Spend Billions Researching Lasers, Weapons of 21st-Century War," *Wall Street Journal*, December 7, 1983, p. 60.
[38] *Pravda*, July 12 and October 27, 1982.
[39] *Pravda*, July 12, 1982.

States intends to sever this interconnection. Should this conception be translated into reality, it would in fact open the floodgates to a runaway race of all types of strategic arms, both offensive and defensive."

Colonel-General N. Chervov of the General Staff has argued that the United States is disregarding the ABM Treaty, Article V of which prohibits the development, testing, or deployment of ABM systems which are sea-based, air-based, space-based, or mobile land-based. Chervov also noted that the use of nuclear explosions to pump x-ray lasers would violate the 1963 Limited Test Ban Treaty and the Outer Space Treaty of 1967.[40]

The openness of the Soviet reaction to Reagan's speech contrasts sharply with the muted character of the Soviet ABM discussion in the late 1960s. The same arguments that Sakharov used in 1967 but which were deemed unsuitable for publication then are now advanced in the Soviet press. Lev Semeiko, for example, has written that

> by completing the planned military programs [in offensive systems] the United States would create a powerful first-strike potential; an ABM defense would follow. And when you have not only an "irresistible sword" but also "a reliable shield," so the hotheads over the ocean reason, why not take a risk and press the nuclear button? . . . Such calculations pose a fatal threat to peace.[41]

The chief reason for this new openness is no doubt that what is being discussed now is a proposed American system, not an existing Soviet one. There has been an ironic reversal: the arguments Andropov has used against Reagan's initiative are precisely those that the Americans used in the late 1960s to persuade the Soviet Union that ABM systems were destabilizing.

By the end of 1983 more detailed Soviet analyses of the issue had been made. In November 1983, a group of Soviet scientists headed by Academician R. Z. Sagdeev, Director of the Institute of Space Research of the Soviet Academy of Sciences and a leading figure in space research, and by Dr. A. A. Kokoshin of the Institute of the U.S.A. and Canada of the Academy of Sciences, issued a report on the prospects for a space-based ABM system.[42] This report examines the technological feasibility of a large-scale space-based ABM system (which is only one of the possibilities being considered in the United States), the potential costs of such a system,

[40] Col. Gen. N. Chervov, interview in *Bratislava Pravda*, April 29, 1983, p. 6 (*Foreign Broadcast Information Service* (*FBIS*), May 3, 1983, USSR International Affairs, p. AA1).

[41] *Krasnaya Zvezda*, April 15, 1983.

[42] *Prospects for the Creation of a U.S. Space Ballistic Missile Defence System and the Likely Impact on the World Military Political Situation*, Report of the Committee of Soviet Scientists in Defence of Peace and Against the Threat of Nuclear War, mimeo, Moscow, 1983.

and the strategic consequences of its deployment. The analysis draws heavily on information published in the West.

The report argues that the creation of a space-based anti-ballistic missile system that could destroy 1,000 ICBMs in their boost phase is beyond current technological capabilities, and would require significant expansion and intensification of R&D work. Even if it could be developed, such a system would be extremely vulnerable to destruction by such means as space mines, retroflectors of laser beams, antisatellite weapons, and powerful ground-based lasers.[43] Various countermeasures—such as shielding missile launchers with reflective and ablative materials—would make it more difficult for lasers to destroy the missiles. The report estimates that it would cost up to $500 billion to develop a system designed to destroy all enemy missiles in flight, while the cost of developing effective means for destroying the orbital ABM systems would be significantly lower.

The report's strategic conclusions follow from this analysis. If a space-based antimissile system is vulnerable to destruction, then it cannot provide effective defense against a first strike, since the attacking side will be able to destroy the system. But such a system might give rise to the illusion that it could provide a relatively effective defense against a retaliatory strike when it would be more difficult to be sure of destroying the ABM systems. The deployment of such a system would therefore have to be seen by the other side as a very threatening move. Under these circumstances, each side—both the side that had an antimissile system and the one that did not—would have an incentive to strike first. Thus the net effect of the deployment of such a system would not be to provide an escape from the relationship of mutual deterrence, but rather to make that relationship less stable. The report notes also that the deployment of such defensive systems would stimulate the development of countermeasures, and thus open up a new channel of the arms race. In the light of these arguments the report concludes that the Soviet Union and the United States should agree to ban the development of space-based antimissile systems. It fails to point out that both countries are already committed, under Article V of the ABM Treaty, not to develop ABM systems or components which are space-based.

In another article, A. A. Kokoshin, one of the group's chairmen, draws attention to the fact that Reagan's speech has evoked severe criticism from leading American scientists, who argue that an ABM system could not be made wholly effective and would therefore have a destablizing effect on

---

[43] "The Soviet Union could deploy antisatellite lasers to several ground sites in the next ten years, . . . " according to Department of Defense, *Soviet Military Power*, 3rd ed. (Washington, D.C.: USGPO, 1984), p. 35.

the Soviet-American strategic relationship.[44] Kokoshin likens the current American discussion to the ABM debate of the late 1960s, thus implying that not only technological and economic, but also political obstacles stand in the way of a realization of the President's vision.

It is possible that these two studies should be understood as part of a Soviet discussion about the appropriate response to the Reagan initiative. In an interview given to Robert Scheer of the *Los Angeles Times*, Academician E. Velikhov, Director of the Kurchatov Institute of Atomic Energy, said that after Reagan's speech he had organized a discussion in the Academy of Sciences. "Its result was very surprising for me," he said. "Not everybody had a real understanding of the issue because rhetorically it is quite attractive to move from offensive weapons to defensive weapons. But the real problem is it's just rhetoric."[45]

Velikhov expressed the hope that the Soviet Union would not copy the United States in trying to develop such a system, but said that it would be hard to resist doing so if the United States went ahead with it. Even if most Soviet experts counselled against it, those who argued in favor would gain the support of the political leadership if the United States proceeded to develop and deploy such a system. Velikhov's argument may be dismissed as no more than an attempt to influence American opinion. But it is a plausible argument, for it is probable, given the Soviet research effort in directed energy, that there are proponents of such systems in the Soviet Union. The history of Soviet nuclear weapons development shows that American R&D has been a crucial catalyst in Soviet R&D activities, and it may be so in this case, too.

For example, it was information about British, American, and German interest in the atomic bomb that impelled Stalin to initiate a Soviet atomic project in 1943. Stalin turned the Soviet project into a crash program in August 1945, once the United States had demonstrated that an atomic bomb was feasible, and immensely destructive. In 1948, after learning of American work on the fusion bomb, the Soviet Union set up a small theoretical group to investigate the possibility of a thermonuclear bomb. In 1952 the American "Mike" test, which produced an explosive yield of 10 MT, led to an expansion of Soviet work on thermonuclear weapons.[46]

The initial Soviet reaction to Reagan's speech has been to portray it as a new threat to Soviet security. Reagan's hints about the possibility of

[44] A. A. Kokoshin, "Debaty v SSha vokrug planov sozdaniya kosmicheskoi protivoraketnoi sistemy" [Debates in the U.S.A. about plans for the creation of a space-based ABM system], *SShA*, 1973, no. 11, pp. 35-46.

[45] Robert Scheer, "A Soviet Scientist on the Real War Games," *Los Angeles Times*, July 24, 1983, pt. IV, p. 7.

[46] See David Holloway, *The Soviet Union and the Arms Race* (New Haven and London: Yale University Press, 1983), pp. 15-28.

sharing the technology were not taken up by Andropov in his statement of March 27, 1983, or by the Soviet media after that. This is not surprising, for the Administration has been vague on this point; besides, the Soviet leaders have been deeply suspicious of the Administration's defense policy. Andropov argued that the attempt to build an ABM system would lead to an arms race in both defensive and offensive systems. All the Soviet commentary, including that which is most skeptical about the feasibility of an effective ABM system, points to the inevitability of Soviet measures to counter an American effort to build an ABM system.

The Soviet Response

There are several steps that the Soviet Union could take in response to an American effort to develop and deploy an ABM system. These are not mutually exclusive. The preceding history shows related Soviet awareness and capabilities.

First, the Soviet Union could develop countermeasures to ensure that its offensive forces could evade, penetrate, or overwhelm the defense. The heavy throwweight of Soviet ICBMs could be used to carry much greater numbers of warheads and decoys than are currently deployed: the SS-18, for example, could carry thirty reentry vehicles, even though it is limited to ten under SALT II. Soviet missiles could be hardened, thus increasing the power requirement for the ABM system's lasers. Long-range cruise missiles, which would not be vulnerable to an ABM system, could be deployed in great numbers. The United States, unlike the Soviet Union, does not have a nationwide air defense system that could be upgraded to deal with this threat. These are just some of the countermeasures that might be taken; others are mentioned in this report.

Second, the Soviet Union could develop the means of destroying the ABM system. Space-based assets would be vulnerable to attack by space mines, antisatellite weapons, ground-based lasers and other systems, while ground-based assets would be vulnerable to nuclear attack by cruise and other offshore missiles. As Colonel-General Chervov put it, "the efforts of one side to form an 'absolute shield' force the other side to reinforce devices for overcoming it, all the more so as the antimissile defense will naturally have its weak, vulnerable spots—in the control, command and targeting system, in the work of the computers and so forth."[47]

Third, Edward Teller has argued that because the Soviet leaders are cautious men, an ABM system would not have to be completely effective to deter them from launching a nuclear strike: if the system were 80 percent effective, they would nevertheless assume it to be 95 percent

[47] Chervov, loc. cit.

effective.[48] In this way the caution of the Soviet leaders would extend the deterrent effect of the system. But if the Soviet leaders believed that the United States had a system that was 95 percent effective, their available course of action would be to take countermeasures to lower that effectiveness, or to increase their offensive forces and adjust targeting plans to ensure that more than 5 percent of a Soviet attack would penetrate, clearly enough to inflict "unacceptable damage" on the United States. In other words, the caution of the Soviet leaders would lead them to exploit all the technical vulnerabilities of the ABM system in order to ensure that they retained the capacity to deliver a "crushing rebuff" (to use the standard Soviet phrase) in the event of a nuclear attack.

Fourth, if the United States appeared to be proceeding toward deployment of an ABM system, the Soviet Union would come under considerable pressure to deploy its own nationwide system, if only to show that it was not falling behind. It might deploy a system based on existing technologies, and then try to supplement it with systems to attack U.S. missiles in their boost phase. It seems that there may be some skepticism among Soviet scientists about the feasibility of an effective ABM system. It is likely, nevertheless, that Soviet work on the new ABM technologies is being speeded up, if only as a precautionary measure.

Fifth, it has been argued by the Administration that demonstrations of American technology would show that the United States was serious about its plan to deploy an ABM system, and would make the Soviet Union more willing to reach arms reduction agreements. This is unlikely, on two counts. First, consider the technology demonstrations of Hiroshima and the "Mike" test (or of Sputnik I or MIRV, for that matter). The effect of these was to spur the other side into further effort, and to remove the brake imposed by uncertainty about the final outcome. This is likely to be the effect of technology demonstrations in this area, too. Second, the prospect that an ABM system might be deployed would make it more, not less, difficult to obtain agreement on the reduction of offensive systems. The Soviet Union would want to retain the capacity to penetrate or overwhelm the defense, and thus would be unwilling to limit the throwweight of its offensive force, or the number of reentry vehicles it could deploy, and might even feel impelled to withdraw from the SALT II Treaty.

It is impossible to be certain now which of these responses the Soviet Union might make, because it is not yet clear exactly what course the American program will take over the next ten to twenty years. It should be clear, however, that the Soviet Union treats the prospect of an American

[48] Craig Staats, "Teller's Plan to Deter War," *The Tribune*, Oakland, California, October 6, 1983.

ABM system as a very serious threat to its own security, and that it has a number of different courses of action to choose from in responding to this threat.

The ABM Treaty and the Stability of the U.S.-Soviet Strategic Relationship

U.S. strategic policy as currently enunciated[49] is in its main lines a continuation of policies developed over the past forty years. Strategic forces are maintained to assure deterrence of aggression, and in this way to preserve strategic stability, prevent nuclear war, and establish a base and incentives for progress in stabilizing arms control and reduction. For these purposes, and for reassurance to Americans and allies, strategic forces equal to and fully as capable as those of the Soviet Union are maintained, constantly modernized, and kept effective.

Such principles are not inconsistent with the main lines of Soviet strategic policy in the Brezhnev era, as just discussed. This convergence enabled some mutual U.S-Soviet understanding on strategic matters, as codified in SALT accords in the 1970s and reflected in their strategic forces.

To an extent not always appreciated, U.S. and Soviet policies on ABM, as reflected in the ABM Treaty and their limited ABM deployments, are at the base of current convergence on approaches to strategic stability, avoidance of nuclear war, and arms control and reduction. It is for this reason that we noted in Section I that the President's SDI raises basic issues regarding U.S. strategic policy that go to the heart of the superpower strategic relationship. This applies both to the President's explicit vision of escape from deterrence through achievement of a defense nullifying strategic nuclear weapons, and to the more modest initial (or alternative) goal of enhanced deterrence through effective, even if partial, ABM defense.

The ABM Treaty is more than a set of limitations on a class of weapons developments and deployments, and it is more than a symbol of hopes for future arms control progress. With its accompanying agreements on offensive systems and on reducing the risk of nuclear war, it has a broader purpose than the specific limitations on strategic arms, valuable as the latter are in themselves. It defines the common premises of the U.S.-Soviet strategic relationship and facilitates pursuit of agreed political measures (including arms control but broader in scope) to avoid nuclear war and its explicitly recognized catastrophic consequences for peoples and civilization.

[49] See for example the report of the bipartisan Scowcroft Commission, *Report of the President's Commission on Strategic Forces*, submitted to President Reagan on April 6, 1983, and endorsed by him on April 19, 1983 (Presidential statement appears in the *New York Times*, April 20, 1983).

It cannot be stressed too strongly that the basic purpose of severely limiting ABM was not to save money, and surely not to achieve "mutually assured destruction." No government has ever had a policy of pursuing mutual destruction. There was mutual recognition during SALT I and at the 1972 Moscow Summit that mutual destruction *could not be escaped* (in that sense, was "assured") if the superpowers were drawn by accident or design into nuclear war. If destruction was to be escaped, the driving purpose of national policy for each had to be *prevention of nuclear war*— which required action by both nations, as well as declarations.

In the belated circumstances in which national leaders came to recognize this imperative jointly, continued existence of prudent but reciprocally constrained deterrent forces had to be accepted by the two sides. The continued existence of these forces carried risks, however, to which the Soviets called attention in their first extended statement at SALT I.[50] The "hot line" and the 1971 agreement to update it, the 1971 agreement on measures to reduce the risk of accidental war, and the 1973 agreement on prevention of nuclear war were all intended to reduce these risks. The first insures that national leaders can communicate with each other if crisis impends, or even at the height of crisis while chances of defusing it still remain. The second commits the two sides to safeguard against accidental or unauthorized use of nuclear weapons, and to provide information to lessen suspicions and misinterpretations, to avoid over-reaction to accidents or ambiguous actions, and to dispose leaders to provide clarifications or corrections before committing themselves to actions which may be hard to stop or retract. The third recognizes that nuclear war might grow out of misunderstood actions of third nuclear powers, or out of military confrontations or other crises, and that in dealing with such situations both superpowers would be conscious of this nuclear dimension and act to avoid it.[51]

Embracing arms control measures but extending beyond them, sustained efforts to improve relations and mutual understanding between the superpowers were envisaged at the 1972 Moscow Summit at which the ABM Treaty was signed. The explicit purpose was to ensure peaceful coexistence, in the face of the tensions, suspicions, and rivalries associated with the differing social and political systems of the two superpowers, and their differing histories and situations in the world. The statement on *Basic Principles of Relations between the USA and the USSR*,[52] also signed at

[50] Smith, op. cit., p. 83.

[51] The texts of these agreements are included in U.S. Arms Control and Disarmament Agency, *Arms Control and Disarmament Agreements: Texts and Histories of Negotiations*, op. cit.

[52] The text of this agreement may be found in Coit D. Blacker and Gloria Duffy, eds., *International Arms Control: Issues and Agreements*, 2nd ed. (Stanford: Stanford University Press, 1984), pp. 429-30.

the 1972 Moscow Summit, sets forth superpower agreement on these points:

> First. They will proceed from the common determination that in the nuclear age there is no alternative to conducting their mutual relations on the basis of peaceful coexistence. Differences in ideology and in the social systems of the USA and USSR are not obstacles to the bilateral development of normal relations. . . .
>
> Second. The USA and the USSR attach major importance to preventing the development of situations capable of causing a dangerous exacerbation of their relations. Therefore, they will do their utmost to avoid military confrontations and to prevent the outbreak of nuclear war. . . .

Such general statements often excite excessive expectations, to be followed by disappointment; this one has been no exception. The quoted principles, nevertheless, are not discredited by the inability of rival nations and their changing leaders to apply them consistently. They remain the only basis on which arms control can progress or have more than a precarious ad hoc effect. And these principles did have one concrete effect on the strategic posture through the ABM Treaty and the limitations it placed on ABMs and their destabilizing consequences.

Thus in its broadest dimension the ABM Treaty is an early milestone of the *political approach* to avoiding nuclear war and its human consequences, and to providing hope and reassurance that, despite the East-West confrontation and the existence of nuclear weapons, nations and their leaders can act to keep nuclear war from erupting. It is a *realpolitik* approach, not an idealistic one. Recognizing differences in ideologies and in political and social systems and their frequently colliding real or perceived national interests, it accepts deterrence as a present necessity and objective condition—not as an active threat, which would be intolerable. In the phrase reiterated by the Soviets in the private SALT dialogue as well as publicly, it is a recognition that, under current conditions for a nation to initiate nuclear war would be tantamount to committing suicide—a sobering and restraining ("deterring") realization.

In that sense deterrence is to an extent prudent, reciprocal *self-deterrence* of initiation of nuclear war, not only a "threat" against an opponent.

Similarly, ABM deployments were severely limited, though not from any antipathy to defending one's nation and population. Initially, ABM development was vigorously pursued on both sides. But responsible leaders, in deciding on their policies and programs, have to look not just at their hopes but to the actual consequences of what they decide to do. From this vantage point, in a world of powerful and diverse nuclear weapons and delivery systems, ABM defense in the late 1960s was found to be not only futile and costly but destabilizing and dangerous. Only by avoiding or actively preventing nuclear war, not by defending against missile attack and thus fighting and winning a war, could nations and people be protected from its catastrophic effects. Further, as the Soviets pointed out at the first sessions of SALT I, characterizing weapons as "offensive" and "defensive" can be misleading. "Offensive" weapons can be *defensive* if used to discourage attack and the outbreak of war; "defensive" weapons can be *offensive* if used to enable an attack to be successful by overcoming defensive or retaliatory efforts.

The rational approach as accepted by both sides in SALT I negotiations and formally confirmed at the Moscow 1972 Summit was thus to give priority to prevention of nuclear war in a context of increasing strategic stability and peaceful coexistence. In such a context, nationwide defense by means of ABM could be relinquished as a dangerous illusion of safety. Taken together, these measures constitute a strategy for managing the nuclear peril which should be recognized and assessed both for its rationale and for its continuing promise as a means of reducing the risk of nuclear war. Its validity can be judged by comparison with other approaches which have been tried.

Since the first manufacture and use of nuclear weapons in 1945, and the prompt though imperfect appreciation of the human consequences of nuclear war as revealed at Hiroshima and Nagasaki, various ways to avoid nuclear war and its consequences have been advocated or tried, even while the constant refinement and multiplication of the weapons have gone ahead.

Thorough-going international control of nuclear activities, culminating in a monopoly by an international organ and eventual elimination of weapons, was proposed in the Baruch plan shortly after World War II. When this proved unnegotiable, elaborate schemes were devised and presented in the 1950s for world-wide conventional and nuclear disarmament that would lead in complex stages to general and complete disarmament (GCD) with elimination of nuclear weapons at the final stages. Also unnegotiable, such approaches were put aside at the end of the 1950s as quixotic in the foreseeable international setting. Although political leaders, East and West, from time to time speak with more or less conviction about the ultimate elimination of nuclear weapons, since the mid-1950s it has been acknowledged explicitly (by President Eisenhower and Soviet leaders of the time) that extensive accumulated stockpiles of fissionable material and facilities for producing it, and the widespread knowledge of how to design and make nuclear weapons, made effective and reliable arrangements for eliminating nuclear weapons difficult to devise and carry out with confidence. The hope of eliminating nuclear weapons remains with us, but not as a near-term solution.

Possibilities of *defense against nuclear attack* were examined and developed in the 1950s and 1960s in the United States and Soviet Union. National leaders, military planners, and defense scientists were naturally reluctant to accept that even in the nuclear age they could not provide the means of shielding their nations and people against attack. Air defenses and civil defenses were adapted to the extent possible to the new conditions of warfare, especially in the Soviet Union. ABM development and initial deployments took on momentum in the 1960s, until parallel reassessments in the Soviet Union and the United States led to their virtual abandonment in the ABM Treaty of 1972.

Mutual deterrence became the bedrock of the strategic relationship. In addition to ABM limits, limitations on numbers and types of offensive systems, and to some extent on their modernization, were pursued in SALT throughout the 1970s: to introduce some predictability into the strategic arms race, to moderate its pace, to channel it where possible into less threatening and destabilizing forms, and then (in the last phases of SALT II and with even stronger emphasis in START) to reduce the opposing arsenals of warheads and delivery systems.

Given the destructiveness of nuclear weapons, however, the prospect of an indefinite posture of mutual deterrence in a setting of political and military confrontation has made increasing numbers of citizens uneasy. Many reject deterrence, or accept it only conditionally, on grounds of morality and humanity as well as high risk, with churchmen and the peace movement most articulate recently. Even dramatic proposals for sharp reductions in nuclear arsenals could not in themselves ease the fear of nuclear catastrophe if nuclear conflict occurred deliberately or by miscalculation: 5,000 strategic nuclear warheads on each side, which would remain, for example, after a 50 percent reduction in current opposing stocks of warheads, could produce the dreaded catastrophe many times over if prevailing suspicions, hostilities, and reliance on weaponry by the superpowers in their dealings with each other were to erupt in their use.

No simple alternative escape route has broad support. A nuclear freeze, widely urged in the United States, is explicitly envisaged as a prelude to further agreed arms control measures—a reversal of direction and change in emphasis, rather than a solution. The thrust of, for example, the recent pastoral letter of the Catholic bishops is similar.[53] Underlying this concern is an impatience with confrontation and competition in which weapons

[53] National Conference of Catholic Bishops, *The Challenge of Peace: God's Promise and Our Response* (Washington D.C.: United States Catholic Conference, May 3, 1983).

and military postures may be marginally regulated but security is seen almost exclusively in national and military terms. What is sought instead is a greater recognition of mutual interdependence; a pursuit of common interests in survival under conditions of diminished anxiety; and a pursuit of peace and international order in which weapons are subordinated to political aims, ways of controlling them are pursued as actively and persistently as weapons improvements now are, and the risks of the continued arms race and military confrontation are given due weight when the risks of arms limitations (in national defense planning no less than in arms control agreements) are debated.

Such a political concept of how the nuclear arms race should be dealt with politically is not novel. Expressed in similar though less idealistic terms, it is the explicit rationale for the SALT 1972 agreements, as stated in the Moscow Summit Communique of May 29, 1972, and in the Preamble of the agreements there referred to. It is customary to be cynical about such pronouncements. Many are indeed made primarily for public effect. Most (and this has been true of the brave words of 1972) have been followed by a period of disappointed hopes.

But there is a difference. The generalities of the Summit Communique were explicitly echoed in the agreements, and the preambular phrases quoted below in turn were reflected in the arms limitations agreed on and carried out. With all the frustrations of subsequent SALT/START negotiations, it is well to bear in mind that the limitations on missile launcher deployments in the Interim Offensive Agreement have been continued on a de facto basis to this day. This provides one fragile but indispensable pillar on which existing limitations on MIRV fractionation and deployment, and on weapons modernization, are founded. It is also a base from which to define reductions. And the ABM Treaty, whose indefinite continuation is now for the first time coming into question, provides even more important constraints—more important because they are grounded more directly and explicitly in the recognition of common vulnerability, and the resultant imperative to act cooperatively in avoiding nuclear war. Some illustrative excerpts may give appreciation of these broader political dimensions of the ABM Treaty and associated agreements:

1. **Joint U.S.-Soviet Communique**, Moscow, May 29, 1972
   Limitation of Strategic Armaments

   The two sides gave primary attention to the problem of reducing the danger of nuclear war. They believe that curbing the competition in strategic arms will make a significant and tangible contribution to this cause.

   The two sides attach great importance to the Treaty on the Limitation of Anti-Ballistic Missile Systems and the Interim Agreement on Certain Measures with Respect to the Limitation of Strategic Offensive Arms concluded between them. . . . Both sides are convinced that the achievement of the above agreements is a practical step towards saving mankind from the threat of the outbreak of nuclear war. . . .

Both sides are also convinced that the agreement on the Measures to Reduce the Risk of Outbreak of Nuclear War Between the USA and the USSR, signed in Washington on September 30, 1971 serves the interest not only of the Soviet and American peoples, but of all mankind.[54]

2. **On-the-Record Congressional Briefing by President Richard Nixon and National Security Advisor Henry Kissinger**, the White House, June 15, 1972

Each of us [U.S. & USSR] has thus come into possession of power single-handedly capable of exterminating the human race. Paradoxically, this very fact, and the global interests of both sides, create a certain commonality of outlook, a sort of interdependence for survival between the two of us.

Although we compete, the conflict will not admit of resolution by victory in the classical sense. We are compelled to coexist. We have an inescapable obligation to build jointly a structure for peace. . . .

In the first round of the talks, which began in November, 1969, the two sides established a work program and reached some tentative understanding of strategic principles.

For example, both sides more or less agreed at the outset that a very heavy ABM system could be a destabilizing factor, but that the precise level of ABM limitations would have to be set according to our success in agreeing on offensive limitations. . . .

. . . the agreement will enhance the security of both sides. No agreement which fails to do so could have been signed in the first place or stood any chance of lasting after it was signed. An attempt to gain a unilateral advantage in the strategic field must be self-defeating.[55]

3. **Preamble to the ABM Treaty**

The United States of America and the Union of Soviet Socialist Republics, hereinafter referred to as the Parties,

Proceeding from the premise that nuclear war would have devastating consequences for all mankind,

Considering that effective measures to limit anti-ballistic missile systems would be a substantial factor in curbing the race in strategic offensive arms and would lead to a decrease in the risk of outbreak of war involving nuclear weapons, . . . [56]

---

[54] U.S. Arms Control and Disarmament Agency, *Documents on Disarmament, 1972* (Washington D.C.: USGPO, 1973), pp. 241-42.
[55] Ibid., pp. 296-300.
[56] See Appendix D.

4. **Preamble to the Agreement on Measures to Reduce the Risk of Outbreak of Nuclear War, September 30, 1971**

The United States of America and the Union of Soviet Socialist Republics, hereafter referred to as the Parties,

Taking into account the devastating consequences that nuclear war would have for all mankind, and recognizing the need to exert every effort to avert the risk of outbreak of such a war, including measures to guard against accidental or unauthorized use of nuclear weapons,

Believing that agreement on measures for reducing the risk of outbreak of nuclear war serves the interests of strengthening international peace and security, and is in no way contrary to the interests of any other country,

Bearing in mind that continued efforts are also needed in the future to seek ways of reducing the risk of outbreak of nuclear war, . . . [57]

5. **Agreement on the Prevention of Nuclear War, June 22, 1973**

Conscious that nuclear war would have devastating consequences for mankind,

Proceeding from the desire to bring about conditions in which the danger of an outbreak of nuclear war anywhere in the world would be reduced and ultimately eliminated. . . .

Article I.

The United States and the Soviet Union agree that an objective of their policies is to remove the danger of nuclear war and of the use of nuclear weapons.

Accordingly, the Parties agree that they will act in such a manner as to prevent the development of situations capable of causing a dangerous exacerbation of their relations, as to avoid military confrontations, and as to exclude the outbreak of nuclear war between them and between either of the Parties and other countries. . . .

Article IV.

If at any time relations between the Parties or between either Party and other countries appear to involve the risk of a nuclear conflict, or if relations between countries not parties to this Agreement appear to involve the risk of nuclear war between the United States of America and the Union of Soviet Socialist Republics or between either Party and other countries, the United States and the Soviet Union, acting in accordance with the provisions of this Agreement shall immediately enter into urgent consultations with each other and make every effort to avert this risk. . . . [58]

---

[57] U.S. Arms Control and Disarmament Agency, *Documents on Disarmament, 1971* (Washington D.C.: USGPO, 1972), pp. 634-35.

[58] U.S. Arms Control and Disarmament Agency, *Documents on Disarmament, 1973* (Washington D.C.: USGPO, 1974), pp. 283-85.

6. **SALT II Treaty,** signed June 18, 1979, unratified

> Recognizing that the strengthening of strategic stability meets the interests of the Parties and the interests of international security . . . [59]

Some of these texts have been almost forgotten. Some—especially undertakings such as Article I of the "Agreement on the Prevention of Nuclear War"—have led to disputes as to interpretation and consistency of conduct. But all are in effect, legally or de facto. Even the ones which seem on reading most at odds with the recent breakdown in routine dealings between the two nations record important perceptions of the limits beyond which rivalry must not be pushed, and are reflected in the actual caution with which both nations approach any direct military confrontation. And they have interesting echoes in the phraseology of President Reagan's version of detente in his recent speech of January 16, 1984[60] on dialogue and constructive cooperation with the Soviet Union, and the realities of international life which demand them.

The words alone can be empty and disillusioning. They are the right words, however; national leaders not noted for their idealism found it important to phrase them and sign them in 1972, and President Reagan found it important to utter similar ones in 1984. At least in the ABM Treaty, the words led to specific actions on strategic weapons which are the most important element of such stability as now exists in the strategic relationship. The Andropov statement of March 27, 1983[61] has a ring of amazement and dismay in its echoes of the ABM negotiations and the 1972 agreements and political understandings which suggests that the ABM Treaty is more than a symbol to Soviet leadership over a decade later. Note might also be taken of the Chernenko statement of March 2, 1984, in which after speaking with regret of aspects of current U.S. policy, he said:

> Relations between powers should be regulated by certain norms. Our idea of these norms is as follows:

---

[59] U.S. Arms Control and Disarmament Agency, *Documents on Disarmament, 1979* (Washington D.C.: USGPO, 1980), p. 190.

[60] "Deterrence is essential to preserve peace and protect our way of life, but deterrence is not the beginning and end of our policy toward the Soviet Union . . . Neither we nor the Soviet Union can wish away the differences between our two societies and our philosophies, but we should always remember that we do have common interests. And the foremost among them is to avoid war and reduce the level of arms. There is no rational alternative but to steer a course which I would call credible deterrence and peaceful competition. And if we do so, we might find areas in which we could engage in constructive cooperation." See the *New York Times,* January 17, 1984, p. 8.

[61] See Appendix B.

- To regard the prevention of nuclear war as the main objective of one's foreign policy, to prevent situations fraught with nuclear conflict. In the event such a danger emerges, urgent consultations should be held to prevent a nuclear conflagration from breaking out.
- To undertake not to be the first to use nuclear weapons.[62]

Many are currently looking for a viable alternative to reliance on purely military deterrence within a confrontational posture, which carries with it intolerable tensions and morally repugnant implications. The political approach to avoiding nuclear war and creating conditions within which this will be possible, summarized in the preceding pages, with the ABM Treaty at the heart of it, is a more clearly defined approach, with more grounding in past U.S.-Soviet dialogue and incipient understanding than any other.

Recent years have not been propitious for such a political relationship between the United States and its major rival in the world. Returning to something like it is not inconceivable, however, on the basis of the President's speech of January 16. One criterion for conduct of the SDI research program might well be to take every precaution not to undercut this possibility.

---

[62] *Pravda*, March 3, 1984.

The SDI and Its Implications for the U.S.-Soviet Strategic Relationship

The SDI: A Technical Appraisal

The Layered Defense

Up to the present, the dominance of offense over defense has been based on technical considerations. In recent years the technology pertinent to this problem has advanced significantly. Great strides have been made in the ability to produce, focus, and aim laser and particle beams of increasingly high power. These new "bullets" of directed energy travel at or near the velocity of light and have led to revolutionary new ideas for defense against ballistic missiles. There has also been a revolutionary expansion in our ability to gather, process, and transmit vast quantities of data efficiently and promptly. This makes it possible to provide high quality intelligence from distant parts of the earth and space in order to assess and discriminate the properties of attacks very promptly—i.e., in "real time." The technical advances in the ability to manage a defense and to attack distant targets very quickly have removed a number of shortcomings of previous defense concepts.

Major technical advances have also led to great improvements in the offense. The crucial question that must be addressed is whether technology now offers a new promise of changing the conditions of offense dominance. Although most agree that we cannot now build an effective defense based on what is known today,[63] can we now foresee the possibility of building an effective defensive system; and if so, under what conditions?

---

[63] Dr. James C. Fletcher, Chairman of the Defensive Technologies Study Team (summer of 1983), whose report has been used by the Departments of Defense and Energy as the technical guidance for the Strategic Defense Initiative, testified that "I would like to say at the outset that no one knows how effective defensive systems can be made, nor how much they might cost." The Fletcher report was concerned with defining a technology development program toward what is "conceivable" for an effective defense. Statement on *The Strategic Defense Initiative*, by Dr. James C. Fletcher before the House Committee on Armed Services, March 1, 1984, p. 6.

The major technical fact that has not changed with time is the over-whelming destructive power of nuclear weapons. To speak, as President Reagan did, of "rendering nuclear weapons impotent and obsolete" by defending one's vital national interests—people, industries, cities—against a massive nuclear attack still requires a defense that is almost perfect. Technical assessments of ABM *concepts* cannot escape this awesome *systems* requirement. If but 1 percent of the approximately 8,000 nuclear warheads on the current Soviet force of land-based and sea-based ballistic missiles succeeded in penetrating a defensive shield and landed on urban targets in the U.S., it would be one of the greatest disasters in all history!

Many components form a defensive system against ballistic missiles, and all are crucial to its effective operation. These include the sensors providing early warning of an attack; the communication links for conveying that information to analysis centers for interpretation, to the command centers with authority to make decisions as to the appropriate national response, and to the military forces to implement the decisions; the sensors of the ABM that acquire, discriminate, track, point, fire, and assess the effectiveness of the attack; and finally the interceptors or directed energy sources that make the kill. The systems for managing the battle and for delivering destructive energy concentrations with precision must be operational at the initiation of an attack and must remain effective throughout. This means being on station, yet being able to survive direct attack. The ability to satisfy these two requirements simultaneously is a major operational challenge. Even if the very ambitious R&D program recently proposed by the Administration achieves all of its major goals, far beyond presently demonstrated technologies, great operational barriers will still remain.

The concept of a "defense-in-depth" has evolved since no single technology alone is adequate to provide an impenetrable defensive shield, or anti-ballistic Maginot Line. This is illustrated in Figure 1 with four layers.[64] The first layer attacks the rising missiles during their boost phase while their engines are burning. Typically, this phase lasts three minutes for modern missiles which are powered by rockets that burn solid fuel, and up to five minutes for liquid fuel boosters. During this time the missile rises above the atmosphere to heights of 200 to 300 kilometers (km). The second (and perhaps third) layer of the defense attacks the warheads, or RVs (reentry vehicles), as well as the post-boost vehicle (which is the small bus that aims and dispenses the individual MIRVs) during their midcourse trajectories lasting about twenty to twenty-five minutes (for ICBMs).

[64] Figure 1 from Clarence A. Robinson, Jr., "Beam Weapon Advances Emerge," *AWST*, July 18, 1983, p. 20.

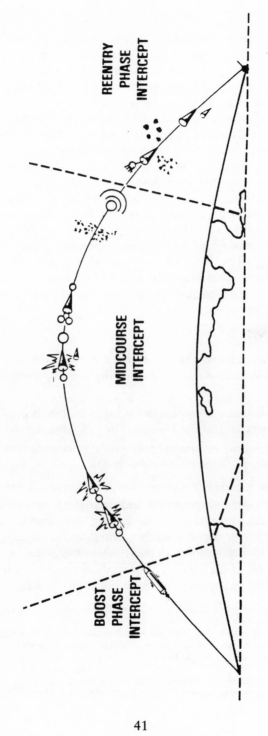

FIGURE 1.

The final or terminal layer of the defense attacks the reentry vehicles during the last minute or two of their flight as they reenter the atmosphere which strips away the lighter decoys accompanying them in mid-flight. A three-layer system, each of whose layers is 90 percent effective, would allow only 8 out of an attacking force of 8,000 RVs to arrive on target and would, if achievable, be highly effective, though less than perfect as a defense. Some of the technologies that have been proposed for a multi-layered strategic defense system are illustrated in Figure 2.[65]

The following subsections will describe the generic technical difficulties that must be surmounted in building such a defensive umbrella. The analysis of the parameters used to characterize specific systems concepts are based on laws of physics and on what is known from open sources. These parameters in no way represent practical or optimal system design numbers. However they are generally very optimistic from the viewpoint of the emerging technology. They are intended to provide "best case" estimates that are useful and valid as a basis for arriving at informed judgments as to the potential practicability of deploying an effective defense against a responsive threat.[66]

Boost-Phase Intercept

The possibility of boost-phase intercept is the principal new element in considering ABM technologies. It also has the highest potential payoff for two reasons:

1. Whatever success is achieved in this initial layer of the defense reduces the size of the attacking force to be engaged by each subsequent layer.

2. If a missile is destroyed during boost when it is relatively vulnerable, all of its warheads and decoys are destroyed with it.

Following the missile boost phase, the defense has more time for performing its functions of acquiring and discriminating warheads from decoys, attacking its targets, and confirming their destruction. On the other hand, although not so severely constrained by very short engagement times, it must also cope with many more objects since a single large booster is capable of deploying tens of warheads and many hundreds of decoys. Thus the two defensive layers for boost-phase and for mid-course

[65] Figure 2 from Clarence A. Robinson, Jr., "Panel Urges Defense Technology Advances," *AWST*, October 17, 1983, p. 17.

[66] Although specific system details are nonexistent and some component concepts may be classified, this is not an issue that need be, or should be, obscured behind an allegation of secrecy. Two studies of defensive technology have appeared recently: Ashton B. Carter, *Directed Energy Missile Defense in Space*, Background Paper prepared for the Office of Technology Assessment of the Congress of the United States, April 1984; Union of Concerned Scientists, *Space-Based Missile Defense* (Cambridge: UCS, March 1984).

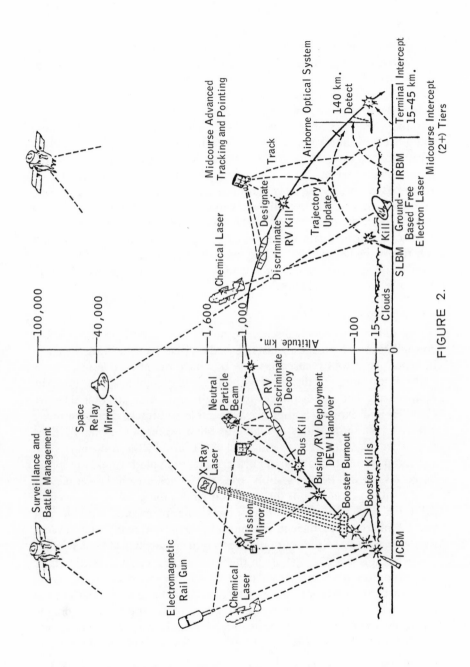

FIGURE 2.

43

intercept face very different technological challenges. Moreover, an effective boost-phase layer, which greatly reduces the number of objects that subsequent layers must analyze, attack, and destroy, is crucial to the overall effectiveness of a defensive system.

In order to illustrate the general problems for boost-phase intercept we consider two types of systems, one with interceptors based in space and the other with interceptors based on ground and ready to "pop-up" on receipt of warning of an enemy attack. A hybrid concept with mixed ground and space basing is also discussed. All defensive systems rely on space-based sensors for early warning; for command, control, and communications; and for overall battle management. The combination of tactics and technology to ensure the survival of the space-based components of a defense against direct enemy attack has yet to be developed. It is listed by the Department of Defense as one of the critical problems that "will probably require research and development programs of ten to twenty years to be ready for deployment."[67]

Space-Based Chemical Lasers

One of the most widely discussed systems for boost-phase intercept is a constellation of high energy lasers based on platforms orbiting the earth in space. Very well focused laser beams have the attractive feature for ABM of traveling vast distances with the speed of light in space above the atmosphere. The disadvantages of space-based lasers are that they are complex and expensive, they are vulnerable to attack, there are many effective countermeasures available to the attacker, and generally their beams are degraded by scattering and absorption by the atmosphere and so they must function above it. Furthermore, each platform of any space-based system will be "on station" over the launch area of Soviet ICBMs only a small percentage of the time as it circles the globe in a low earth orbit; i.e., each platform will have a large "absentee ratio." Therefore, it will be inherently inefficient, having to be replicated many times over if the defense is to provide continual protection against ICBM launches.[68]

Chemical lasers that operate in the infrared (IR) region, emitting high energy continuous beams of coherent light of several microns (μ) wavelength are candidates for such a system. Their technology has matured to the point that one can foresee achieving high levels of power, reasonable efficiency, and very well focused beams. We can illustrate the requirements for such a system by extrapolating this technology far beyond what has

[67] *Defense Against Ballistic Missiles: An Assessment of Technologies and Policy Implications* (Washington D.C.: U.S. Department of Defense, March 6, 1984), p. 29.

[68] In order to avoid this it would be necessary to achieve effective operating ranges from geosynchronous orbits at an altitude of 36,000 km. This is not a practical prospect.

been demonstrated today to what is believed to be attainable in practice. Let us first calculate the kill potential of such a laser against an ICBM booster during second-stage burn starting about one minute following launch when it has risen above most of the atmosphere. The range will increase with the output power of the laser and with the quality of the optical system in creating a well-focused beam; and this range will decrease if the target is hardened against higher values of energy per unit area which are required in order to cause thermo-mechanical damage to the relatively thin skin of the booster. If the laser output is expressed in terms of a power, P, and if the beam has an angular divergence, Θ, so that

its spot size at range, R, has grown to an area of approximately $\frac{\pi}{4}\Theta^2 R^2$, then the energy deposited in a time interval, Δt, onto a unit area of the booster surface, which is known as the fluence, F, will be

$$F = \left[\frac{4P\Delta t}{\pi\Theta^2 R^2} \right] \tag{1}$$

In order to destroy the booster, F must be greater than the so-called kill fluence, F_K. The combination of factors $(\frac{4P}{\pi\Theta^2})$ in Equation (1) is called the brightness and characterizes the performance of the laser itself.

It is possible to deliver F_K to larger distances, R, and in shorter times, Δt, if we make the beam divergence, Θ, as small as possible. In turn this will mean that fewer lasers, and less fuel to power them, will have to be orbited in space in order to provide continual coverage against a massive missile attack. There is, however, a theoretical lower limit to the angular divergence due to the wave nature of light. This is the diffraction limit, Θ_d, and is given approximately by[69]

$$\Theta_d \simeq \frac{0.8\,\lambda}{D} \tag{2}$$

where λ is the wavelength of the laser light, and D is the diameter of the mirror which focuses the light onto its target. In order to get an idea of the numbers involved, consider a hydrogen-fluoride (HF) chemical laser with a wavelength of 2.7 microns. High powers and efficiencies have been demonstrated for continuous wave operation of such lasers. For focusing, consider an optically perfect 4-meter diameter mirror so that the diffrac-

---

[69] The full diffraction angle that defines the angular width of the spot from minimum to minimum is given by $\frac{2.4\lambda}{D}$. Equation (2) is close to the width of the region in which most of the beam energy is concentrated. It defines the full width at half maximum intensity of the diffraction spot.

tion limited value of the beam spread according to Equation (2) is $\Theta_d = 0.54 \times 10^{-6}$ radians.

We also envisage a power output of 100 megawatts (MW) as an ambitious and feasible goal for a chemical laser in the IR region of the spectrum for orbiting into space. Our assumptions of 100 MW power output and of 4-meter-diameter main optics performing at the diffraction limit correspond to a system whose brightness is 4.4×10^{20} watts per steradian. Such a high value of brightness is more than an order of magnitude beyond the level currently envisaged for technology demonstration during the 1980s[70] and will require major technical advances. In testimony before the Senate Armed Services Committee on March 23, 1983, the day of President Reagan's speech, Major General Donald Lamberson, head of the Pentagon's program on directed energy weapons, referred to a 4-meter optical configuration as a very large system that has not been constructed before, much less operated at or even near its diffraction limit.[71]

To continue this illustration we must specify the kill fluence. It is envisaged that boosters can be hardened to withstand the thermo-mechanical effects of a fluence of 20 kilojoules (kJ) delivered within a short time interval (several seconds) to one square centimeter of their surface[72] ($F_k = 20$ kJ/cm^2). At a range of 1,500 km the beam spot size in the optically perfect laser system described above will be approximately 0.5 square meters (obtained by calculating $\frac{\pi}{4} (0.54 \times 10^{-6} \times 1{,}500 \text{ km})^2$) corresponding to a power density of 20 kW/cm^2. It thus takes one second to deliver a kill fluence of 20 kJ/cm^2 at this range. During this time of one second, the missile will travel about 7 km along its path and the laser beam will have to track it accurately in order to hold the beam spot on the same part of the booster as it advances. To do this will require an aiming and tracking accuracy better than used above for intercept. Published reports

---

[70] It is intended to demonstrate 2 MW chemical IR laser in 1987 and scale upward to 10 MW "almost immediately" and to demonstrate beam control of 4-meter segmented optics in 1988. See Robinson, loc. cit.

[71] There have also been occasional references to design goals of a 10-meter diameter main optics with a 10 MW laser, corresponding to a brightness of 2.8×10^{20} watts per steradian, slightly smaller than in our example. Although the power level of the laser presents a more modest goal, that of an optically perfect 10-meter optical system which is rapidly steerable is much more ambitious.

[72] Boosters of present day missiles are typically rated as being able to withstand fluences of ~ 1 kJ/cm^2 delivered to the few-millimeter-thick skins of their boosters. Slight increase of their skin thickness by a fraction of a cm layer of heat shield material such as carbon is one ready way to increase hardness to the value used in the text. The added weight of the heat shield (about 6 kilograms per square meter of surface area) could be offset by a relatively small reduction in missile payload (for example by deleting one of the RVs on an SS-18).

in $AWST^{73}$ indicate that the report of the Fletcher Committee recommends the demonstration of an aiming accuracy from space systems of better than 10^{-7} radians by 1988. This will require major technological advances.

With the above reference parameters we can now compute the total energy that must be orbited in space and the total number of laser battle stations that are required to form an effective defensive layer against a maximum ICBM attack from the Soviet Union. For each ICBM attacked at a range of 1,500 km, a total energy of about 100 MJ must be expended. In order to defend against the current total Soviet force of 1,400 ICBMs in an all-out launch against U.S. targets, a minimum of 140×10^9 joules (140 GJ) is needed.

Much more energy than this must be lifted to space orbit, however. As they circle the earth most of the lasers in a constellation of defensive satellites will be far beyond their maximum effective kill range from the ICBM launch areas. In addition, more than one laser must be within kill range in order to attack all 1,400 Soviet ICBMs, whenever and however they may choose to launch them, before they complete their boost phase. To illustrate, let us assume that our conceptual 100 MW laser system can, within two seconds, acquire, track, aim, attack, assess damage, attack again if necessary, and realign and stabilize its optics to its next target. This means that one laser at most can destroy something like ninety missiles, assuming that the boost phase lasts for three minutes at altitudes above most of the atmosphere (engagement time), i.e., above 15-20 km. Thus, no fewer than sixteen laser platforms must always be "on station" above the Soviet ICBM launch area.

Since the earth is rotating under the orbit of the laser stations, many more satellites will have to be orbited in order to ensure that there are always sixteen within range whenever the Soviets might choose to launch their ICBMs. Characteristically a laser with a 1,500 km kill range is on station 5 percent of the time[74] over the Soviet launch areas and therefore a total of $16 \times 20 = 320$ laser battle stations is the minimum number required for constant coverage against a massive ICBM attack.

With the assumptions of this example it is necessary to lift a total energy into orbit for powering the lasers of 20×140 GJ. Thus, even with very optimistic assumptions about what can be achieved *in principle*, one finds

[73] Robinson, loc. cit.

[74] (revised from original report) This corresponds to four planes of thirteen satellites each, separated by 3000 km at the latitudes of the Soviet ICBM fields, and with between two and three always within kill range. These are only rough numbers for the constellation size as derived above, but very similar results follow from a more detailed quantitative analysis. For the same input parameters, the "on station" percentage is higher and the maximum laser brightness is lower (by factors of approximately two). These differences offset one another, and in any event are small compared to uncertainties in our highly optimistic assumptions.

that 6,000 tons of fuel must be lifted into orbit to power such a constellation of hundreds of lasers.[75] This requirement adds up to more than 250
shuttle loads of fuel alone.[76]

This then gives a general idea of the scale of a space-based laser system,
although the specific numbers given are sensitive to assumptions about
kill ranges and laser performance according to Equations (1) and (2). For
example, had we assumed that the boost phase was shorter, the required
number of battle stations would be larger.[77] If the engagement time is
reduced from three to two minutes, which would be the case for modern
solid fueled ICBMs, the required number of lasers increases from 320 to
480.[78] The number would also increase with further hardening of Soviet
boosters. *AWST* reported that the Fletcher panel called for an increase of
the demonstrated capability of the HF laser to 2×10^{22} watts/steradian in
order to counter anticipated hardening of boosters by the Soviets.[79] The
currently quoted demonstrated brightness is 10^{15} watts/steradian, so that
an increase by a factor of more than ten million is being called for. Our
illustrative example assumed a brightness of 4.4×10^{20} watts/steradian.
The expense and complexity of a space-based laser system is further
emphasized in testimony presented to the Senate Armed Services Committee by Major General Donald Lamberson:

> A constellation of space laser platforms might by themselves . . . possess the
> capability to negate, say 50%, of a large scale ICBM attack on U.S. strategic
> forces by engaging several hundred missiles in boost phase as the first layer of a
> ballistic missile defense-in-depth.[80]

[75] HF is a very efficient high power laser. Its specific energy is 1.4 kJ per gram (gm) of fuel
or at 33 percent efficiency 500 J/gm. To provide 2,800 GJ requires, therefore, some 6,000
tons of fuel.

[76] This number is obtained by using a mean between the 30-ton shuttle load for an east-
west orbit and 15-ton for polar orbit. According to *AWST*, the Fletcher committee has
recommended that to make a layered defense a viable option, the U.S. must expand its space
transportation system to provide a capability to launch about 100 tons to medium altitude
orbits tens of times a year. See Clarence A. Robinson, Jr., "Study Urges Exploiting of
Technologies," *AWST*, October 24, 1983, p. 50.

[77] It would be smaller had we assumed less than one second was required for acquiring,
tracking, aiming, and assessing damage in addition to the one second dwell time for the laser.

[78] As discussed later, modern technology permits the boost phase to be reduced even
further to no more than one minute of burn, with only minor reductions in efficiency of the
missile. This tactic and technology would drastically increase these numbers and is another
difficulty for space-based lasers as an effective boost-phase layer of defense.

[79] Clarence A. Robinson, Jr., "Shuttle May Aid in Space Weapons Test," *AWST*, October
31, 1983, p. 78.

[80] *Strategic and Theatre Nuclear Forces*, Hearings before the Committee on Armed
Services, op. cit., p. 2651. Mistakenly declassified congressional testimony by the Defense
Department in 1981 indicated that a "damage denial" space-based chemical laser system
would cost $500 billion (in 1981 dollars). See Charles Mohr, "Space Lasers Might Stop Half
of Missile Attack, Experts Say," *New York Times*, March 31, 1983, p. 20.

Note that General Lamberson is referring to an attack by just a portion of the current Soviet ICBM force. We also have no idea of a practical system at this time because, as General Lamberson remarked, the advanced concepts (lasers, particle beams, and high power microwaves) are only in the early technology stage: "We are walking down a path unfolding the physics and exploring concepts demonstrating technology. . . ."[81]

There are additional generic difficulties for any defensive system for which components are predeployed in space. In addition to specific countermeasures that render them ineffective, their foremost difficulty is that they will most likely be vulnerable to direct enemy attack. Among the simplest direct threats that could be deployed even during the early stages of building up to a full space-based defensive layer are small and relatively cheap space mines with conventional explosives. They could be launched into orbits, and detonated by radio command from ground to damage the large, delicate, and highly vulnerable optical parts. The presence of such space mines would not be covert. They could "shadow" a satellite in a manner similar to that used by ships on the high seas; in particular by Soviet intelligence-gathering ships (which also may be armed) that currently observe our naval battle groups. Of course, the Soviets could also put nuclear bombs in orbit. These would have an enormous range for damage of such systems and their necessarily "almost perfect optics." Ground-based laser beams pose another direct threat to the sensitive optical sensors of such a system. The space-based defenses would have to be prepared to "blink" if so attacked in order to avoid damage, particularly if the incident radiation comes in short, intense pulses.

Not all laser platforms would have to be attacked and put out of action; just a sizable fraction of that small percentage that are on station over the ICBM launch areas during boost phase. The offense can then be confident that a sizable fraction of his attack will penetrate the first layer of the defense. In considering the difficulty of making such space-based systems survivable, it is important to recognize that they are much more delicate (and expensive!) than the individual ICBMs against which they are deployed and, therefore, the task of protecting them is inherently more difficult than that of hardening the ICBMs against them.[82]

Countermeasures other than direct attack include further hardening of the missiles against the incident beam energy to a level somewhat higher than the 20 kJ/cm^2 assumed in the above example. Two approaches are to

[81] *Strategic and Theatre Nuclear Forces*, Hearings before the Committee on Armed Services, op. cit., p. 2646.

[82] As stated by General Lamberson in his testimony on March 23, 1983: "It is much easier to kill a satellite than it is a strategic aircraft, and doing that is much easier than killing a ballistic missile." Ibid., p. 2647.

coat the booster by a somewhat thicker (by a few millimeters) heat shield, or dispense an aerosol to absorb the incident fluence and disperse it harmlessly. Another useful technique is to spin the missile at the rate of a few turns a second during boost so that the beam energy is distributed at lower fluence around the booster surface. There are additional problems that can be created for such a defensive system. Precursor nuclear bursts at high altitudes can precede an attack and disrupt its operations, particularly its sensors and communication links. There is, of course, no spare time available for replacing or reconstituting these components since the entire system must operate within the first few minutes in order to destroy an ICBM during boost phase. After boost is completed, the targets are, or can be made, harder and thus require a greater fluence to destroy; and once the MIRVs are deployed they are not only much harder, but there are many more of them as targets. The defensive system can also be decoyed by false targets consisting of bright rockets and other hot sources simulating the missile exhaust.[83] And, if the history of MIRVs has anything to teach, it is that, faced with such a prospective defense under development and test, the Soviet Union could simply increase its arsenal of offensive missiles and warheads in order to maintain its deterrent. (At $5 to $10 million per warhead, the Soviets could buy a lot of warheads before equaling the DOD estimate in 1981 of $500 billion for a space-based laser defense.)

In the final analysis, a very extensive and expensive constellation of chemical lasers predeployed in space appears to offer no credible prospect of forming an effective defensive layer against a large scale attack at the current high levels of the threat.[84]

"Pop-Up Systems": Ground-Based X-Ray Lasers

In an effort to avoid most of the problems just described, the defense may choose not to predeploy in space, but to "pop-up" from the ground when alerted to an attack. The individual battle stations of such a system will have to be launched instantly as a missile payload. Thus, they must be

[83] Such rockets would have to appear like the ICBMs themselves, but would be much less expensive since they would carry neither warheads, MIRVs, buses, nor accurate guidance systems; nor would they have to be launched from underground silos.

[84] In testimony, on May 2, 1983, to the Senate Armed Services Committee, Edward Teller, a leading proponent of a strong strategic defense, dismissed the practicability of such a system as follows: "I believe we should not deploy weapons in space, and in this sense to talk about starwars is a most inappropriate description of what the main question is. To put objects into space is expensive . . . infrared lasers, the presently known chemical lasers, do not seem to me to fulfill the basic requirement of a good defense, and that is that the defense must be considerably less expensive, must require considerably less effort than the offsetting effort in offense." *Strategic and Theatre Nuclear Forces*, Hearings before the Committee on Armed Services, op. cit., p. 2898.

substantially smaller and lighter than the infrared chemical lasers we have been describing, each one of which required about one shuttle load of fuel. Therefore, we must consider beam wavelengths much shorter than the micron range, since the wavelength of the light sets the scale size of the optics for a well-focused beam. Furthermore, a lighter and more compact energy source is required. This suggests that we consider x-ray wavelengths which are 100 to 1,000 times shorter than the IR wavelengths of microns. The criteria of shorter wavelength and compact energy source both suggest an x-ray laser pumped by a nuclear explosive, which is a candidate system.

Therefore, we turn now to a consideration of a "pop-up" system consisting of x-ray lasers, driven by nuclear explosives, and mounted onto a missile that can itself be launched very rapidly upon receipt of information of an enemy attack. By itself, a nuclear explosion releases a very large amount of energy which is not focused, but which emerges in all directions. However, if a sufficiently large fraction of the energy from the nuclear explosion can be used to drive one or more lasers, and thus be focused into very highly collimated beams, it can cause severe impulsive damage to objects at very great distances. The gain, G, of such a system is defined as the product of two factors. The first is the degree of focusing as expressed by the ratio of 4π, the full solid angle of a sphere, to the solid angle into which the beam is focused, as expressed by $\pi(\Theta/2)^2$ where Θ is the angular divergence of the beam due to optical diffraction. The second factor is the efficiency, η, which is the fraction of energy in the explosion that is converted to laser energy. This gives

$$G = \eta \frac{4\pi}{\pi(\Theta/2)^2} \tag{3}$$

If one can achieve an overall gain of, say, 10^4, the destructive range of an explosion will be increased by 10^2, or the square root of the gain.

Examples cited in Russian literature,[85] as well as published American reports,[86] give some idea of gains that may be achieved in practice. First of all, how good a collimation might one achieve? The Soviet reference describes focusing into one milliradian or $\Theta = 10^{-3}$ corresponding to a gain of $G = 2 \times 10^7 \eta$. The theoretical limit of focusing from a laser rod is

[85] See, for example, F. V. Bunkin, V. I. Derzhiev, and S. I. Yakovlenko, "Specification for Pumping X-Ray Laser with Ionizing Radiation," *Soviet Journal of Quantum Electronics*, vol. 11, no. 8, July 1981, pp. 971-72.

[86] See, for example, Raymond C. Elton, Robert H. Dixon, and John F. Seely, "X-Ray Laser Pumping and Charge Transfer," *Physics of Quantum Electronics*, vol. 6, 1978, p. 243; Michael A. Duguay, "Soft X-Ray Lasers Pumped by Photoionization," ibid., vol. 3, 1976, p. 557; and G. Chapline and L. Wood, "X-Ray Lasers," *Physics Today*, June 1975, p. 40.

given approximately by the square root of the ratio of the wavelength of the laser light to the length of the laser rod[87]—that is:

$$\Theta_{min} \simeq \sqrt{\frac{\lambda}{L}} \simeq \frac{3 \times 10^{-5}}{\sqrt{E_{kev}}} \simeq 3 \times 10^{-5} \sqrt{\lambda_{nm}}$$

where we have set the rod length L = 1 meter and introduced E_{kev} as the energy of the laser photons measured in kilovolts, or λ_{nm} as the laser wavelength in nanometers (10^{-9} meters). At the diffraction limit, the maximum gain for a laser rod of length L meters is

$$G \simeq 2 \times 10^{10} E_{kev} L \eta$$

As to current thinking about gains that are practical, *AWST* reports that the Fletcher report has recommended demonstrating by 1988 the technical feasibility of focusing 10^{16} joules of x-ray energy into a unit solid angle (1 steradian).[88] This criterion is considerably lower than a theoretical limit, and in more familiar terms, means the following. In an explosion of a 150 kiloton (kT) bomb—which is the limit allowed for underground tests by the Threshhold Test Ban Treaty of 1974—a total energy of 5.4 x 10^{14} joules is released into all directions, or 4π steradians. Assuming 75 percent of the energy is released in x-rays, this corresponds to radiating 3.3 x 10^{13} joules per steradian. What has been proposed as a technical goal for 1988 is thus equivalent to an increase by a factor of 300 for the focused yield from a 150 kT source. Such an increase would effectively increase its kill-range by about a factor of 17.

Open U.S. and Soviet scientific literature has analyzed and discussed different materials and physical conditions for pumping x-ray lasers. For example the kinds of x-ray lasers the Soviets discuss include pumping transitions in zinc and iron in a plasma under appropriate physical conditions so that there will be a population inversion between several excited levels (for example, the fifth and the fourth and the fourth and the third excited levels). A number of lasing transitions with energies from tens of electron volts (eV) up to a kilovolt (keV) have been discussed.[89] The corresponding wavelengths of the coherent radiation vary between one-tenth and one-thousandth of a micron. With powerful and compact sources such as nuclear explosives, and with short laser wavelengths in the x-ray region, it is feasible to mount this kind of system on a rocket to be boosted into space upon detection of a missile attack.

[87] This is achieved by matching the geometric spread from a rod of length, L, and diameter, d, i.e., d/L, with the spread due to diffraction, λ/d.

[88] Robinson, "Panel Urges Defense Technology Advances," op. cit., p. 17.

[89] P. L. Hagelstein, *Physics of Short Wavelength Laser Design*, Ph.D. thesis, Lawrence Livermore National Laboratory, 1981.

The kill mechanism in this case is impulsive damage due to ablative blow-off, caused by a very short intense pulse of incident energy, in contrast to the thermal heating by the chemical laser. The maximum kill range will depend on the gain that can be achieved in practice as well as the required kill fluence. This technology is still very immature,[90] but we shall assume here that there are no operational limits posed by limits in gain.

In considering the possibility of a practical "pop-up" system of this type, the most difficult and important operational issue to address is whether it can be deployed sufficiently rapidly even to attempt a boost-phase intercept. Modern ballistic missiles complete their powered flight, or boost phase, within three to five minutes after launch. At that point the remaining target becomes the post-boost vehicle consisting of the individual warheads and the "bus" on which they are mounted. The bus, which is considerably smaller than the booster, has its own internal guidance and power system for altering its path in order to drop off the individual warheads on their different trajectories. This means that a pop-up system, designed for boost-phase intercept, has itself only a few minutes available to be boosted to a high enough altitude above the atmosphere in order to be able to initiate an attack. In practice an x-ray laser can only operate at altitudes above 100 km. X-rays of 1 kev energy and lower are absorbed by the atmosphere at lower altitudes.[91] Thus a defensive x-ray laser would have to be launched literally within seconds of the launch of an initial enemy attack.

Furthermore, such a "pop-up" system would have to be based far off shore from continental U.S. soil, and near to Soviet territory. Otherwise, due to the curvature of the earth, it will be impossible for the x-ray laser beams to "see" the booster above the horizon before the end of burn. This operational constraint is illustrated in Figure 3 (see p. 54). The attacking missile is typical of current solid fuel ICBMs (and SLBMs) which complete boost in less than four minutes following launch and at altitudes below 250 km. The x-ray beams from the laser-interceptor must themselves always remain above the atmosphere. For example, if its distance from an attacking ICBM at an altitude of 200 km is as large as 3,000 km, a 1 kev

[90] It is reasonable to assume that a comparable level of fluence is required to destroy a booster by impulsive kill as by thermo-mechanical damage as discussed in the analysis of the chemical lasers. In order to deliver $20kJ/cm^2$ to a range of 1,500 km, the brightness of an x-ray laser will have to be increased by a factor of 10,000 beyond the goal reportedly recommended for demonstration in 1988 by the Fletcher committee.

[91] The minimum altitude is even higher for lower energy x-rays since the absorption coefficient increases by a factor of 2^3 for each decrease by a factor of 2 in x-ray energy. The minimum altitude can be raised even higher by nuclear precursor explosions at high altitudes that are properly designed to heat the top of the atmosphere, thereby causing it to expand and rise.

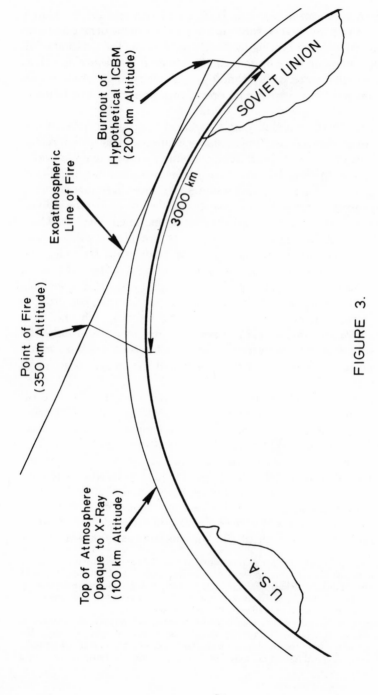

Point of Fire
(350 km Altitude)

Exoatmospheric
Line of Fire

Burnout of
Hypothetical ICBM
(200 km Altitude)

SOVIET UNION

3000 km

Top of Atmosphere
Opaque to X-Ray
(100 km Altitude)

U.S.A.

FIGURE 3.

x-ray laser itself must rise to an altitude above 350 km within the three minutes available to attack. This poses a severe requirement for a very high thrust booster for launching the laser defense. This defensive concept also requires that the command and control chain must operate almost instantaneously over great distances—and do so, after the first shots, in a heavily disturbed nuclear environment. Furthermore, the sensors to acquire, track, discriminate, and assess target damage must also operate accurately and reliably in a nuclear disturbed environment. Evidently such a system would have to be, essentially, entirely automated for quick response. This poses serious policy problems because the automated processes would necessarily include authorized release of nuclear weapons, as well as decisions as to whether and how to respond, depending on the intensity and tactics of the attack. For example, since an x-ray laser can fire only once, destroying itself in the act, should it be launched against a single attacking ICBM, or only against a suitably large barrage?

In addition to these formidable operational requirements, there are two technically available countermeasures by the offense that can *deny any possibility* of a pop-up x-ray laser defense.[92] The first countermeasure is simply to redesign the offense with new high-thrust "hot" missiles that complete their burn at altitudes below the top of the atmosphere. Unclassified studies[93] presented to the Fletcher panel calculate that the penalty in payload due to such rapid burn, lasting only about one minute, is no more than 10 to 15 percent. A second countermeasure is to alter the trajectory of the launch, depressing it so as to complete its burn below 100 km. Thus even if we assume that x-ray laser systems are successfully developed with sufficiently high gain—many orders of magnitude beyond current technology—to look promising for destroying boosters at long range, the offense can use the opacity of the atmosphere to defeat them with missiles of high thrust that complete their boost before they can be attacked.

Hybrid System for Boost-Phase Intercept

Other technologies and systems concepts have been proposed in an effort to escape the drawbacks of space-based and "pop-up" systems. One such concept that has been widely discussed is that of a system of ground-based lasers whose beams are aimed up to a small number of large relay mirrors in synchronous orbits at 36,000 km altitude. These relay mirrors at high altitudes then direct the beams to various mission mirrors, orbiting

[92] These countermeasures also deny the possibility of basing x-ray lasers in space for boost-phase intercepts.
[93] Briefing on "Short Burn Time ICBM Characteristics and Considerations," to the Defensive Technologies Study Team by Martin Marietta Denver Aerospace, with supporting backup analyses, July 20, 1983.

earth at lower altitudes from which they are redirected on to their targets. This concept is also illustrated in Figure 2 (see p. 43).

This hybrid system avoids three of the problems of a space-based laser defense: 1) fewer of its parts have to be protected from direct attack in space; 2) its ground-based lasers do not have to be replicated many times over in order to compensate for the large absentee ratio for lasers circulating in low earth orbits; and 3) it is not necessary to shuttle large amounts of fuel into orbit. It also avoids the very severe problem of time constraint for boost-phase intercept that is encountered by pop-up systems. However it faces several severe and unavoidable technical and operational challenges. First, the large focusing mirrors which are high value and crucial nodes of the system remain vulnerable in space. Also the directed light beams must travel very great distances, 36,000 km up and 36,000 km back from the relay mirrors in geosynchronous orbit. Therefore by Equation (2), large optics and short wavelengths are necessary to reduce the diffraction and keep the energy focused on such a long path from laser to target.

The technologies under study for this hybrid system rely on pulsed lasers of the excimer or free-electron type with wavelengths in the one-fourth to one-third micron range which is smaller than that of chemical lasers (such as HF) by a factor of about ten. Since this light must be transmitted through the atmosphere without attenuation, it is shifted to the blue end of the visible spectrum (of 0.5 micron wavelength; this is accomplished by passing through a hydrogen Raman cell).

This concept necessarily relies on "active optics" in order to compensate for the effects of atmospheric turbulence that cause scattering and defocusing of the directed light beams (in a similar manner to which distant stars are seen as disks and jitter). "Active optics" means the following: a weak laser beam from space shines to ground and its beam spread is analyzed as a measure of local atmospheric turbulence, which is then compensated by use of deformable focusing mirrors for transmitting the beam from the ground-based laser. This technology, although still immature, has been progressing rapidly and, in principle, can achieve the goal of transmitting highly focused beams through the atmosphere.[94] In addition to atmospheric compensation there is the problem of weather, and in particular of cloud cover absorbing the laser energy. This requires replicating the ground-based lasers at widely distributed sites in order to have

[94] In his speech to the Council on Foreign Relations in Washington, D.C., Dr. George Keyworth, the President's Science Advisor, claimed that "we've also seen very recent advances that permit us to compensate for atmospheric break-up of laser beams." Dr. George Keyworth, *Reassessing Strategic Defense* (Washington D.C.: Council on Foreign Relations, February 15, 1984), p. 12.

a high probability that an adequate number are free of cloud cover; or of basing the lasers high near mountain tops above the clouds.

We refer back to Equations (1) and (2) (see p. 45) for a comparison of the parameters of this hybrid concept with the earlier discussion of space-based infrared lasers. The requirement here is to deliver a kill fluence more than forty times as far as the range of 1,500 km used in that example. Let us assume that the optical system has a 10-meter diameter. Since we are now transmitting light of one-half micron wavelength at the blue, or short wavelength end of the visible spectrum, the diffraction limit in Equation (2) is forty nanoradians, or one-thirteenth that in the earlier example. By Equation (1), this extends the range for the same kill fluence by a factor of thirteen, leaving another factor of more than three to be gained somewhere in order to achieve the same fluence as in that example. One approach would be to increase further the diameters and thus reduce the optical diffraction of the laser sources, the relay mirrors, and the mission mirrors. Alternatively, the product of the power output times the kill time, $P\Delta t$, in Equation (1) must increase about an order of magnitude, i.e., by a factor of 3^2. This requires either very intense pulses of 1,000 MJ energy, or multiple pulses for the booster kill.

Even assuming that the technical goals are achieved, there still remains the operational problem of the vulnerability of the few large relay, and the mission, mirrors in space. They and the ground-based laser stations are reminiscent of the large phased-array radars of the earlier generation of ABM systems at the time of SALT I which proved to be their "Achilles heel." It has yet to be specified or understood how the small number of large and delicate mirrors in space, and of ground-based installations, can be protected with confidence.

Other Concepts for Boost-Phase Intercept

Another, somewhat more exotic, concept is that of using particle beams for directed energy weapons. Electrically neutral matter (atomic beams in particular) can travel large distances without being deflected by the earth's magnetic field, and is effective in depositing its energy within targets for destroying them. This is a very immature technology, however, much less advanced than the laser beams we have considered, and very little can be said about the practicality of orbiting operationally effective accelerators in space.[95] Large accelerators in space would of course be vulnerable to direct attack, as are any space-based systems. Like laser stations they

[95] To quote from General Lamberson's testimony of March 23, 1983, to the Senate Armed Services Committee: "Particle beam technology is currently the least mature of the directed energy technology efforts." See *Strategic and Theatre Nuclear Forces*, Hearings before the Committee on Armed Services, op. cit., p. 2653.

would be more fragile to attack as well as more expensive than their targets—the ICBMs.

Directed energy weapons that are sources of high power microwaves have also been mentioned among the concepts for strategic defense. They too are in a very early stage in which the basic physics is still being studied, particularly with regard to how high a power can be achieved and how well it can be focused. It is too early to offer even educated guesses about their potential effectiveness, particularly against countermeasures, including shielding the targets against their radiation.

Finally, we mention the possibility of a boost-phase defensive layer that relies on material interceptors such as small missiles or pellet screens, launched from a constellation of space-based battle stations. Such "high frontier" proposals have been advanced as potentially being ready for deployment sooner than the more exotic directed energy beams.

Destruction of the target is achieved by the kinetic energy impinging on the booster when it encounters a high velocity interceptor or a cloud of matter in the form of debris or pellets. However, such schemes have been generally judged as ineffective for boost-phase intercept on grounds of time constraints, countermeasures, and vulnerability.[96]

Mid-Course Intercept and Battle Management

The concept of a defense-in-depth envisages one or two layers operating during the mid-course phase, which for ICBMs lasts twenty to twenty-five minutes following the completion of the booster burn and prior to reentry of the warheads into the atmosphere. During the first few minutes of mid-course the post-boost vehicles will be targets before and while they are

[96] This view was expressed in response to questioning by Dr. Robert Cooper, Director of DARPA during his testimony to the Senate Armed Services Committee on May 2, 1983. He indicated that such "high frontier" concepts do not provide a cost effective potential for ballistic missile defense and could be countered at relatively low cost by the offense. We can illustrate their problems by considering the constraints on delivering the interceptors from their space-based platforms against the rising missiles before booster burn-out. Assuming a 200 second burn time for the booster and a typical closing speed of 10 km/sec (7 km/sec is orbital speed for low earth orbits), the maximum interceptor range is 2,000 km. Thus the absentee ratio for such a system will be high, comparable to what we saw earlier in our analysis of space-based chemical lasers. Furthermore, since each interceptor can attack only one booster, no fewer than 25,000 interceptor rockets will have to be launched into space on many hundreds of battle stations. The weight of each rocket will be typically several or more tens of kilograms as required to propel a projectile whose weight, including its homing sensors and divert rockets for final maneuver to impact with its target, will be several kilograms or more. This leads to a total system weight well in excess of 1,000 tons that has to be lifted into space. If the offense counters such a deployment with shorter burn times, the required size of the defensive tier would increase further. Finally these large space platforms share the vulnerability of all extensive space-based systems to direct enemy attack. See *Strategic and Theatre Nuclear Forces*, Hearings before the Committee on Armed Services, op. cit., p. 2891. For the most complete description of the "high frontier" concept, see Lt. Gen. Daniel O. Graham, *High Frontier* (Washington, D.C.; 1982).

dispensing the individual warheads. Thereafter the surviving warheads are, individually, the targets. Although the time constraints are less severe, there are other factors that increase the difficulties of mid-course intercept. The post-boost vehicles are generally more difficult to destroy than are the boosters, since they are much smaller and harder to track; also they can be designed to be harder and to release the MIRVs very rapidly. The warheads are much smaller and harder still since they must withstand extreme stresses due to deceleration and due to heating up from atmospheric friction as they slam back into the top of the atmosphere. They are also far more numerous. In addition each missile may dispense hundreds of light decoys which follow the same paths in the absence of friction above the atmosphere as do the warheads.

While it is true that the capacity to analyze and transmit data has increased greatly in recent years, so has the size and sophistication of the offense—as well as its ability to confuse the defense. The offense can, for example, resort simply to anti-simulation to confuse the sensors and stress, if not saturate, the data-handling capacity of the defense. Anti-simulation is the technique of making warheads look like decoys which can be dispensed in very much larger numbers with little weight penalty. One means to do this is to enclose the warheads in balloons with several thin metal-coated layers so that all balloons have the same appearance, whether or not there is a warhead inside. Additional severe difficulties can be caused by precursor detonations of nuclear weapons. The infrared radiation from the air heated by high-altitude nuclear explosions creates a severe background—known as "red-out"—against which the sensors of a proposed mid-course ABM layer must operate and "see" the warhead.

As described in Defense Department documents,[97] the different layers of a defensive system would operate semiautonomously with their own sensors and data processing, as well as weapons and rules of engagement. As part of the overall battle management—i.e., monitoring, allocating the available defensive systems, assessing the results of the attack, and refiring if necessary—data would also be passed to successive layers in the defense. Input data from the sensors must be organized and filtered to see which objects can be discarded and which are candidates for further analysis— leading to tracking, attacking, and assessing damage. An effective boost-phase intercept that clears away close to 90 percent of the threat is thus very important in making the battle management and data-handling problems more tractable, and hence in achieving an effective strategic defense.[98]

[97] See, for example, *Defense Against Ballistic Missiles: An Assessment of Technologies and Policy Implications*, op. cit.
[98] In its summary of the Fletcher report, *AWST* describes the mid-course sensor constellation in a layered defense as consisting of 100 satellites, each weighing 20,000 kg for discrimination, precision tracking, and target designation. See Robinson, "Study Urges Exploiting of Technologies," op. cit., p. 50.

No viable concept has yet been demonstrated or devised for a highly effective mid-course defense against a massive threat of many thousands of warheads plus many times more decoys.[99] The critical needs include not only a battle management software that far exceeds anything accomplished so far in complexity and difficulty,[100] but also the ability to protect all the critical space-based components, including many sensors, against enemy attack, whether from space mines, debris clouds, direct-ascent antisatellite weapons, or directed energy weapons (lasers) on ground or in space. Furthermore, to contribute to a mid-course defensive layer, these critical elements must survive throughout the entire time of the engagement up to final atmospheric reentry of the attacking warheads.

The directed energy systems described earlier for boost-phase intercept (chemical lasers based in space, or "pop-up" ground-based x-ray lasers) are also candidates for a mid-course defense. Although they would no longer face the severe time constraint of a boost-phase intercept, they face the operational problems we have just described. The entire system—including intelligence, communications, and surveillance satellites and the optical and directed high energy components, whether on ground, in low-earth orbit, or at synchronous altitude—must survive and operate in a hostile environment for many minutes in order to engage the threat. Moreover, each individual warhead—as well as the many additional decoys—will have to be attacked, and the warheads are generally much harder targets requiring a substantially larger kill fluence or impulse. Therefore, the overall energy requirements are greatly increased beyond

[99] The following exchange during the Senate Hearings on May 2, 1983, between Senator Warner and the Director of DARPA, Robert Cooper, emphasizes the importance of the battle management problems. See *Strategic and Theatre Nuclear Forces*, Hearings before the Committee on Armed Services, op. cit., p. 2892.

Senator Warner: What in your view is the single greatest factor limiting our actions in the field of space-based ballistic missile defense? Is it financial resources or technological uncertainty?

Dr. Cooper: I think basically it is the technological uncertainty that we face in this general area. I think the single thing that we have not focused attention on in the past, which may represent the most stressing technological problem, is the complexity of any comprehensive battle that we would have to wage against a large-scale strategic missile attack.

It is the battle management problem, if you want to characterize it that way. Currently we have no way of understanding or dealing with the problems of battle management in a ballistic missile attack ranging upward of many thousands of launches in a short period of time.

This is the problem that we would face in the projected threat environment that the Soviets could project against us.

[100] The first conclusion of the Battle Management, Communications, and Data Processing panel of the Fletcher Committee Report (vol. 5) was: "Specifying, generating, testing, and maintaining the software for a battle management system will be a task that far exceeds in complexity and difficulty any that has yet been accomplished in the production of civil or military software systems."

the severe requirements already established in our earlier illustrations of boost-phase intercept.

Terminal Defense

The terminal layer of the defense takes advantage of the atmosphere to slow down and strip away the lighter decoys accompanying the warheads in free space during mid-flight.

The requirements for a terminal defense of hardened military targets such as missile silos and command posts are much simpler and more readily achievable than for a strategic nationwide defense. Intercept can be made successfully much nearer to a target that is itself both small and hardened to withstand very high levels of overpressure. In addition, the goal of such a hard site defense is not to destroy all incoming warheads, but only enough of them to cause the attacker to expend more of his force than he destroys.

Improved technologies in recent years have enhanced the prospects for a cost-effective hard site defense that operates standing alone without prior layers of the defense. Important advances include interceptors that achieve much higher accelerations; improved accuracy that raises the possibility of nonnuclear kill; and sensors that can discriminate warheads from decoys at higher altitudes. Whether a hard site defense of a missile silo will, in reality, exact an "entry price" of two or three, or as many as six or seven attacking warheads per hardened target, is sensitive to many quantitative assumptions. The point to emphasize, however, is that hard site defense, whatever its potential and genuine merits, is very different from a goal of a nationwide defense designed to render nuclear weapons "impotent and obsolete." As such, it should be debated on its own merits.

The requirements of a terminal layer of a strategic defense of the nation are much more severe than for hard site defense since the urban-industrial targets are much larger and more vulnerable, and have much higher value. Standing alone, a terminal defense offers no prospect of defending the nation against a massive attack. This conclusion was reached during the earlier ABM debates of 1969-70, and the new technologies have added little to alter it. If, however, a terminal defense operates behind effective boost-phase and mid-course defensive layers which remove all but a few percent of the attack, the conclusion may be different. In particular, with improved sensors and interceptors, the defense may engage the incoming warheads at higher altitudes and contribute to limiting damage to the targets being defended. A terminal defense may thus limit damage as the final tier of a partially effective defense-in-depth.

Overlap with Other Forms of Strategic Defense

The ABM Treaty attempted to deal with the problem of "SAM upgrade" or, more generally, the problem that air defense systems or anti-tactical ballistic missile systems, or their components, might have some potential capability against strategic missiles. Since that time, new forms of the "SAM upgrade" problem have emerged as a result of technical advances. The sophistication of tactical aircraft and of strategic bomber armaments (now including air-launched cruise missiles or ALCMs), of land- or sea-based cruise missiles, of intermediate-range missiles (such as SS-20s and Pershing IIs), and of tactical missiles have continued to increase. Efforts to defend against aircraft and cruise missiles have led to modern generations of air defenses with improved radars, computers, and high-acceleration interceptors with growing potential to defend against these shorter range missiles. Moreover, intermediate-range ballistic missiles on 1,000 to 2,000 mile trajectories generally fly at lower speeds than longer range strategic missiles. This increases the time available for the defense to attack them in the terminal phase. Work is underway both in the Soviet Union and the United States to try to exploit this possibility of theatre, non-strategic ABM. Ways of updating the ABM Treaty to take account of this new form of the "SAM upgrade" problem will have to be addressed in future reviews of the Treaty.

Antisatellite Technology (ASAT) and Defense vs. Defense

ASAT is a much simpler technical problem than ABM defenses that operate above the atmosphere (exoatmospheric ABM), since the targets are softer, fewer, predictable both in their position and time, easier to discriminate, not easily replaced, and have communication and control links from earth that can be attacked. There is no question about the technical feasibility of ASAT systems that will be effective against satellites in low-earth orbit in the near future. Extending ASAT effectiveness to synchronous orbit altitudes of 36,000 km and higher will be a technical challenge, but presents no fundamental problems.

The significance of ASAT for strategic defense lies in the threat it poses against the space platforms of the ABM, in particular against the warning, acquisition, and battle management sensors. On the other hand, the significance of the Strategic Defense Initiative for ASAT is that it will spur technical developments that, inevitably, will be threatening to the critical communication and early warning satellite links on which a ballistic missile defense must rely. This presents an unavoidable dilemma: ASAT threatens ABM, but ABM developments contribute to ASAT.

More generally, ABM deployments will pose threats to each others' defensive systems, and in particular to the space-based components. This introduces the prospect of defense as an adjunct of a first strike. For example, a pop-up x-ray laser system launched as part of an attack can contribute to the overall advantage of a first strike by contributing to the suppression of both the defense and the retaliatory strike.

Technical Summary

There have been major technological advances in recent years, but we do not now know how to build an effective nationwide strategic defense against ballistic missiles. This is true whether the goal is to transcend deterrence with a nearly leakproof defense or to enhance it with an effective but partial defense. It is true against the current Soviet threat—and there is no present prospect of achieving such a defense against an unlimited offensive threat that can overwhelm (i.e., more MIRVs and warheads); evade (i.e., fast burning "hot" boosters and cruise missiles whose flight paths lie entirely within the atmosphere); or directly attack the defense. As Dr. Richard DeLauer, Under Secretary of Defense for Research and Engineering, said to reporters on May 17, 1983, "With unconstrained proliferation, no defensive system will work."[101] Many years, if not decades, of research are required before we can begin to proceed from imaginative concepts, crude ideas, and estimates to educated guesses. If the system is to meet the President's stated goal of rendering nuclear weapons "impotent and obsolete," not only must it work to almost 100 percent perfection, managing an enormous task of battle management in very short times, but it must do this the very first time that it is used. No realistic shakedown tests are conceivable, especially in the nuclear environment the system will encounter in a real engagement.

The Report of the President's Commission on Strategic Forces (Scowcroft Commission) that was released in April 1983 stated that:

> At this time . . . no ABM technologies appear to combine practicality, survivability, low cost, and technical effectiveness sufficiently to justify proceeding beyond the stage of technology development.[102]

Dr. Cooper, Director of DARPA, endorsed this conclusion in his May 2, 1983, testimony to the Senate Armed Services Committee.

In addition to the technical and operational challenges, there are also very serious political questions raised by the President's speech and by an intensified R&D effort aimed at altering the U.S.-Soviet strategic relation in a very fundamental manner. It is to these important considerations that we now turn.

[101] Richard Halloran, "Higher Budget Foreseen for Advanced Missiles," *New York Times*, May 18, 1983, p. 11.
[102] *Report of the President's Commission on Strategic Forces*, April 6, 1983, p. 12.

The SDI: Possible Outcomes and Their Implications for Deterrence and Stability

The current SDI program is directed toward two related objectives and possible outcomes:

1. President Reagan's vision of essentially leakproof defenses which would nullify and even make obsolete nuclear weapons and their threat to humanity.

2. As an interim or alternative outcome, an imperfect but substantial nation-wide ABM defense which raises the uncertainty and costs of undertaking a nuclear attack, and saves lives if one occurs.

Pursuing these objectives, it is argued, is likely to enhance deterrence, increase stability, and improve prospects for arms control.

As we have seen, the program and its objectives bring into question some of the fundamental assumptions of U.S. defense policy and U.S.-Soviet relations.[103] What will be the consequences of pursuing the SDI, and of renewed ABM deployments? Are there risks and dangers to be recognized and weighed along with the hopes and goals of the program's supporters?

During recent decades, other goals for ABM deployment have been proposed, and different types of ABMs have been considered or even undertaken. In this section we analyze five possible outcomes of the new defense initiative, assessing their possible value and risks:

1. The SDI program as proposed.

2. Local ABM defense of high-value targets (probably hardened, hence "hard site defense" or HSD) such as ICBM silos or key command and control facilities.

3. A "thin" ABM defense against one or a few attacking missiles, either from a small nth nuclear power, or launched by accident or miscalculation.

4. An asymmetrical outcome with either the United States or the USSR, but not both countries, achieving a substantial ABM defense.

5. ABMs are not deployed competitively by individual nations. Instead, a decision on deployment is deferred until the arms race has been brought under control and major reductions in the offensive forces are effected. Subsequently, ABM deployments will be undertaken by mutual agreement only if judged likely to enhance stability and confidence.

[103] The President's Commission on Strategic Forces (Scowcroft Commission) in its final report observes: "Ballistic missile defense is a critical aspect of the strategic balance and therefore is central to arms control . . . no move in the direction of the deployment of active defense should be made without the most careful consideration of the possible strategic and arms control implications." *Report of the President's Commission on Strategic Forces*, March 21, 1984, p. 7.

The SDI Program

In the year following the President's speech, studies organized by the Department of Defense, and policy discussions within the administration, have produced the FY 1985-89 SDI program summarized in Appendix C. The President's vision of a radical shift from offense to defense in the strategic balance is still spoken of with optimism: Dr. Keyworth, the President's Science Advisor, cites "truly remarkable advances" in relevant technology, which he judges to "offer the possibility of a workable strategic defense system." He summarizes the conclusions of the hundreds of experts who examined the problems and possible solutions as being that "they now believe the President's objective is not an unrealistic goal, and they conclude it probably could be done."[104]

ABM research will continue. Such work is justified both as a "hedge" in the current precarious state of U.S.-Soviet relations, and as one area of basic science directed toward understanding the concepts and processes underlying modern weaponry and their potentialities and limitations. Moreover, the human longing to escape from living indefinitely under the threat of nuclear destruction is both natural and strong; and the possibility that revolutionary new technologies can help find a path to such an escape, however implausible, cannot be ruled out *a priori*.

But premature adoption of uncertain but possibly illusory concepts can make the nuclear dilemma worse, and more difficult of solution. ABM deployment has already occurred in the past. However, it has been severely limited so as not to imperil stability and raise the risk of war. As we assess the promise of new technologies, we must never lose sight of the conditions under which they could enhance deterrence and stability rather than imperil them. The President's vision of a shift from offense dominance to defense dominance cannot happen overnight. There will necessarily be a long transition period of partial defense, and so it is most important to analyze the implications of an "effective" though imperfect defense designed to enhance deterrence.

The SDI concept entails a mixed offense-defense strategic posture, with a layered ABM defense capable of destroying a large part of the incoming missiles in a massive attack. Faced with such a defense, which in prudence an attacker would probably have to assume might be even more effective than it actually would be, it is argued that the benefits of a first strike would be so marginal as to reduce drastically any temptation to launch one.[105]

---

[104] Keyworth, op. cit., pp. 11-13.
[105] Fred S. Hoffman, *Ballistic Missile Defenses and U.S. National Security*, Summary Report prepared for the Future Security Strategy Study, October 1983, p. 2.

Is this simple scenario plausible? Could it happen, and would the results of U.S. ABM development and deployment be so straightforward and clearly beneficial?

It is not enough to make a strong case that, with novel technology, we can heavily diminish an attack by the presently estimated Soviet missile forces. The Soviet Union will not remain passive; nor would the United States in a similar position. One should be wary of "the fallacy of the last move."

As we undertake an expanded R&D effort toward deploying defenses we must look not just at our achievements but also at the *net* consequences as the Soviets, during the many years required for R&D testing and deployment, develop their own response to a major redirection of U.S. strategic doctrine. Who can doubt that, following the President's speech and commitment to a major new defense initiative, the Soviets are thinking even now of the prospect that the United States might succeed as an outcome of a massive effort? To the extent we succeed in deploying an effective but imperfect defense, what we are challenging in the first instance is not just the Soviet incentive to a first strike, but the efficacy and reliability of their retaliatory deterrent forces which they count on to deter a U.S. first strike. They will look at the emerging U.S. mixed defense-offense posture to judge whether the United States remains vulnerable to, and deterred from initiating, nuclear war. In so doing, they will apply the test put vividly during SALT I and in other Soviet statements: *does the United States still recognize that to start a nuclear exchange would be for it to commit suicide?*

Some Soviets, citing U.S. speeches about avoiding nuclear war, might argue that U.S. motives in ABM deployment are purely peaceful and humanitarian; but others will point to ongoing U.S. strategic programs to modernize and strengthen our offensive striking power. They can also point to the emphasis (e.g., in the Scowcroft Commission report) on the importance of accurate reliable ICBMs such as the MX missile in order to validate the U.S. nuclear guarantee of NATO Europe under NATO's flexible response policy which relies on the option of first use of nuclear weapons.[106] They will note that the President's March 1983 speech stressed that " . . . as we proceed, we must remain constant in . . . maintaining a solid capability for flexible response." If only as worst case conclusion, it will be argued that the United States might be intending now—or might decide in a crisis—to undertake a first strike relying on its ABM to deal

---

[106] *Report of the President's Commission on Strategic Forces*, April 6, 1983, p. 16.

with a diminished Soviet response,[107] holding its effects to tolerable levels (tolerable to some strategic planners even if not to the U.S. population itself).

Thus the first likely Soviet response will be to assess—probably on the worst case basis—what reduction in the effectiveness of their retaliatory strike the prospective U.S. ABM system might exact. The directive to Soviet strategic planners will be to give first priority to countermeasures to enhance the penetrating ability and size of survivable Soviet retaliatory forces so that an intolerable level of devastation could still be assured in response to any U.S. first strike or to any exaggerated calculation of the effectiveness of the ABM. Marshal Ogarkov has emphasized as recently as December 5, 1983,[108] the Soviet determination and capability to maintain retaliatory power in the face of any future U.S. strategic program.

Can the Soviets succeed in such a response? In all analyses to date of the relative cost and time required for the retaliatory offensive forces to outpace ABM defense and retain the previous damage capability against soft targets—cities, industrial areas, soft military targets—advantage has clearly rested with the responding retaliatory forces. If such cost estimates were to shift in favor of the defense, one factor in the equation would be changed. However, there is no reason evident as yet to anticipate any change in that conclusion.

Protecting our society in the event of nuclear exchange *by any means other than preventing nuclear war* remains an illusion, in view of the uncompromising reality of the number and power of nuclear explosives and the diversity and substantial survivability of delivery means. Since this hard reality exists—and should be apparent—for the leaders of both superpowers, a deliberate first strike could be grimly rational only if the Soviet leaders could persuade themselves that U.S. retaliatory forces could be attacked and destroyed with sure effect and subsequent impunity. Is an extensive but imperfect U.S. ABM deployment the right way to reduce any Soviet temptation to act on such an expectation?

As the Scowcroft Commission demonstrated, the plausibility of any such Soviet attempt at a disarming strike now is small, in view of the diversity of U.S. strategic forces and deployment modes and the high level of survivability of a substantial majority of the warheads they carry. Actions to increase that survivability, now being pursued, can move ahead more quickly and surely, and less ambiguously in Soviet eyes, than development and deployment of a large ABM system.

---

[107] In this sense a partially effective defense can be used as an effective part of a nation's offense, and an adjunct of a first strike policy. As all are aware "a leaky umbrella is of greater value in a drizzle than in a downpour."
[108] *Pravda*, December 6, 1983.

If there is an interim role for ABM in protecting ICBMs, a dedicated hard site defense (discussed in the next sub-section) is the more promising means, faster, more directly undercutting any first strike incentive, and presumably cheaper (though so far not judged worth the cost). Such an ABM system would have a better chance of avoiding the broader destabilizing effects of a nationwide ABM defense.

There is one other basic factor. A U.S. ABM deployment is not likely to go unmatched by the Soviet Union. The result of both nations moving toward a mixed defense-offense could be reciprocal, and could reinforce fears of first strike. Strong disincentives to deliberate initiation of a nuclear exchange would still remain on the partial defense hypothesis we are now examining—imperfect defenses mean levels of casualties and damage on both sides that would be tolerable only on Strangelovian calculations. But the real risk of nuclear war does not lie in a cold-blooded decision to initiate one. It is what might happen under the pressures and suspicions of a crisis—an accidental triggering of a nuclear incident, miscalculation, or loss of control by responsible leaders. ABM on both sides would exacerbate the risk; each could fear that the other would calculate his situation to be better (however bad) if he struck first, and would then benefit from relying on his ABM defense only to deal with a weakened response.

No agreement exists or is likely among Sovietologists regarding the circumstances that might lead the Soviet Union to have recourse to nuclear attack on the United States. Most U.S. military leaders have, however, discounted the likelihood of a "bolt from the blue"—a coolly calculated effort to achieve military superiority by a bold disarming strike. The more plausible situation would be a mounting crisis, in which both sides would wrestle with the fear that the opponent might strike first on rational or irrational calculation of advantage. And in the face of the apparent inevitability of nuclear war, a preemptive strike could appear better than awaiting the adversary's initial blow. There are grounds in Soviet military writing for taking this scenario as one which their strategic policy has contemplated. If this is so, then the kind of "enhanced deterrence" under examination here could actually increase the incentive, although it is not likely to be the determinant. The preemptive strike would be made not on any calculation of absolute advantage, but solely on one of *relative* advantage: since a nuclear attack is inevitable anyway, strike first in order to enhance one's own effectiveness and diminish the enemy's as much as possible.

No definitive conclusion can be reached in the abstract about "enhanced deterrence" from a mixed defense-offense strategic force. If one looks at the history of Soviet-American strategic competition, it is difficult to believe that either side would let the other deprive it of a retaliatory deterrent capability. If the concern is with deterring a first strike, it is equally difficult to be confident that a constructive difference would result. A mixed defense-offense posture designed to deprive the opponent of a first strike capability is itself likely to look—in motivation and in capability—uncomfortably like a first strike posture. This would be true, particularly, of a space-based ABM system, where the fragility and vulnerability of the space-based components would make them a poor reliance except in support of a preemptive strike.

Section IV will examine further the impact of a mixed offense-defense strategic posture on strategic stability and arms control prospects, and whether there are simpler, surer, and less costly ways to enhance deterrence, stability, and arms control progress.

Whatever the other doubts about the value of a partially effective defense, there is attraction to the argument that, to the extent that some of the attacking missiles are destroyed, it would lessen damage and save lives. Is this a realistic calculation, or is it wishful thinking?

There is reason to doubt that much reliance should be placed on a partially effective defense to protect urban industrial areas and people in the event deterrence fails and a nuclear exchange occurs. For such soft targets, not many nuclear warheads need penetrate in order to exact massive devastation and casualties. If only a fraction of the attacking warheads get through, the catastrophic consequences for people and property will be immense.

But will not whatever is saved be worth the cost? Here, we must objectively assess whether there will be an actual saving. Proponents of ABM argue that, even if it is only partially effective, a potential attacker will be conservative and attribute substantial capability to the defense which faces him. This is the argument for enhancing deterrence. But here we are considering what value ABM would have if deterrence fails and an attack is made. In that case too, the attacker will calculate his requirements conservatively, and program more warheads in his retaliatory punitive strike than are actually needed to achieve whatever level of destruction is judged necessary. It is thus a grim prospect that, for soft targets, at least as many casualties and as much damage will follow a partially effective ABM defense effort as without it.

The only way to save lives from a nuclear exchange is to avoid nuclear war, by deterrence and other political and arms control measures to enhance stability and preserve peace. The prime test of ABM is how it supports such efforts—and that test is not favorable to ABM.

Finally, note that these reservations regarding the value of a mixed offense-defense posture for enhancing deterrence apply equally to a nearly leakproof defense in its initial and middle stages. Such a system with its

69

complexity and scale cannot be quickly constructed. It will be subject to countermeasures, especially in its early stages; it will face offensive increases and enhancements; and it will be paralleled by a Soviet ABM program challenging our deterrent forces. Such a combined offense-defense competition does not augur well for assured deterrence or stability.

ABM Defense of Point (Hard Site) Targets

Until recently, U.S. ABM research and development within provisions of the 1972 ABM Treaty has given priority to technology for defense of ICBMs or other hard targets. The technology developed for the planned Safeguard ABM system, and deployed and operated briefly in the early 1970s at Grand Forks ICBM field, has matured considerably. Other concepts including nonnuclear kill of incoming warheads by swarms of attacking pellets or by dust clouds raised by buried nuclear bombs have also emerged. Whether improvement has reached the point at which it would be cost-effective to mount local ABM defense of ICBMs or other high value targets such as command posts or communications facilities would need case-by-case analysis. It would depend on the mode of deployment of the offense and on the value of the individual targets: for example, a single-warhead Midgetman missile would be a much less rewarding target than a MIRVd fixed large ICBM.

Such hard site ballistic missile defense (BMD) deployment is not *in principle* inconsistent with the ABM Treaty. The principal consideration there is that local ABMs not be so numerous or so configured, or use technology with such broader capabilities, that a base would be laid for a broad area defense of the country. If unambiguous local BMD deployment seemed attractive, and in principle consistent with the Treaty, some modifications or agreed interpretations of the 1972 Treaty and 1974 Protocol might be needed. But they might not be too difficult to work out if the longer-range implications of resuming limited deployments could be fully understood, agreed upon, and taken account of in the modifications and the subsequent deployments. If these conditions cannot be satisfied for militarily attractive local ABM deployments, the United States separately and the two nations in interaction could face a difficult decision: Which is more advantageous, the ABM status quo or unilateral changes with resulting uncertainties as to military and political stability? Here again, there are other approaches to enhancing stability.

Thin ABM Defense Against Small Attacks

The concept of a "thin" ABM defense to cope with one or a few missiles, either from a small nth nuclear weapons state, or an accidental or unauthorized launch, poses the issue of the acceptability of a nationwide infrastructure facilitating relatively quick deployment of an ABM defense of the nation. Such a thin defense would have all the structure and components of a thick ABM, would give experience in construction and operation, prove out key components, and establish a potential production base. It would raise fears of clandestine production or preparatory steps toward broader deployment, and complicate verification. These are not necessarily insoluble difficulties, but they would require weighing and solution if a "thin" ABM is not to negate the goals of the Treaty.

Efficient terminal and mid-course ABM defenses could cope with small attacks; that was the stated prime purpose of the first Sentinel U.S. ABM program in the 1960s. But since small attacks could be directed at high-value urban industrial or military centers anywhere in the nation, a widespread, even if "thin," ABM system would be required. In addition to cost, the issue of building a base for a thick system would be posed inescapably by a layered defense beginning with boost-phase intercept.

Even if a thin ABM could be designed and deployed without undermining other requisite ABM constraints, it is far from clear that it could achieve its purpose or that its cost would be justified. Nth countries (beyond the present major industrial nuclear powers) or terrorists are not likely soon to have strategic ballistic missiles; their delivery systems are more likely to be ships, aircraft, or clandestine means of emplacing weapons.

ABM defense against small or accidental Soviet launches raises questions regarding command and control and ABM decisionmaking processes. These are not trivial questions. Will there be a requirement for strong evidence of a major attack? What are its susceptibility to spoofing and the costs of error? Indeed, activation of ABM defenses in times of tension could itself have escalatory effect, especially if subject to interpretation as a precursor of a preemptive attack.[109]

There are alternative ways in which to address the risk of accidental or unauthorized nuclear launches. For example, disarming "override" command devices in offensive missiles, activated to defuse or destroy them at a sufficiently responsible level in the command chain, might be installed unilaterally or by mutual agreement as a preferable alternative to actuating ABMs.

We can ask whether the value of a thin ABM system against small attacks can justify its installation in whole or in large part. This use of ABM seems inadequate to be a decisive consideration. If deployment would reinforce deterrence or add in any other way to the stability of the U.S.-Soviet strategic balance, then the additional benefit of use against

---

[109] These command and control questions are particularly troublesome for an automated system relying on boost-phase intercept, as discussed earlier in this Section.

small attacks would not be needed as justification. If deployment is destabilizing, it is hard to see how the potential gain against small attacks could reverse the assessment. Furthermore, the cost appears prohibitive if current order-of-magnitude estimates have any validity.

Asymmetrical Outcomes

It would be ironic if the outcome of the current official U.S. revival of interest in old as well as novel ABM deployment concepts is for the United States, once it recognizes technical realities, to do nothing in the end except continue R&D, while the Soviet Union actually builds its preferred ABM system. This possibility emphasizes the need for complementing our internal debate about ABM with appropriate dialogue with the Soviet Union, rather than proceeding only unilaterally.

It is highly unlikely that either the United States or the Soviet Union could long proceed toward a substantial ABM deployment without the other moving to match it in some form. Small asymmetries are not ruled out, so long as "equal rights" obtain. This is shown by the existing situation in which only the Soviets have a limited operating system around Moscow. Similarly, so long as the overall strategic balance seemed stable, even considerable differences in the sophistication of competing ABM systems would be acceptable, if at times irritating, as they are today for respective SLBMs, ICBMs, and intercontinental bombers. However, very advanced technology on one side might be more destabilizing, at least until its net effectiveness could be confidently assessed.

Fears of Soviet breakout, based on their experience with the existing Moscow deployment and the upgradings of radars and other components which have been observed there and elsewhere in recent years, are frequently voiced. Soviet activities have to be monitored and compliance with the ABM Treaty confirmed to protect the U.S. against the possibility of breakout. It is important and useful for the U.S. to challenge—and demand correction of—Soviet transgressions. However, undue alarm is not warranted. No Soviet activities currently jeopardize the broad-based U.S. deterrent. Moreover, Soviet breakout cannot quickly undermine the overall U.S. deterrent. In a sustained ABM race, the U.S. industrial base and relevant technology could overcome and surpass any Soviet initial advantage from the first move. It is a different and more basic question to ask what U.S. ABM deployments would do for U.S. security and the effectiveness of deterrence, and whether other measures would serve these ends more cheaply and surely. Improved penetration aids—rather than matching the Soviet ABM actions directly—may be the best U.S. response either to a thin Soviet ABM system or additional regional/local Soviet ABM deployments. This is especially true as the survivability and flexibility of U.S. strategic forces improve. Yet, as already observed above, it may be psychologically difficult for U.S. leaders to accept a Soviet deployment not matched in kind—and there will be enough real or self-appointed experts to find alarming Soviet motives or capabilities in any program they undertake.

If some ABM deployments become imperative as political reassurance, it is desirable, and should be possible, to avoid gestures and to minimize costs and potential instabilities by proceeding with only those deployments that are designed to perform precise missions contributing to strategic stability, even if not mirroring Soviet programs. Thus, given other asymmetries in our forces and capabilities, it should be possible to respond (for example) to a thick Soviet ABM around Moscow that exceeds the agreed SALT I limits with a U.S. combination of advanced penetration aids and diversified delivery systems plus some ABM point defense of high value sites. Such offsetting deployments would carry their own tensions and pressures for further deployments, but might be less destabilizing than more open-ended matching competitive ABM programs.

Moving to ABM and Defense Dominance after START

Given agreed and sturdy limitations on offensive systems, together with U.S. and Soviet confidence in mutual compliance, a basic concern about the SDI would in theory be voided. In theory—for the hypothesis just stated is a radical one. Strategic arms control can confidently be expected to serve well in reinforcing the stability of a mutually satisfactory strategic balance, and in facilitating progressive limitations and reductions in offensive arms. So long as deeply rooted rivalry persists between the Soviet Union and the United States, however, even successful arms control agreements will be subject to constant tension and strain. Each side will continue to rely on deterrence by placing ultimate reliance for prevention of nuclear attack on its residual offensive forces. Even if the technical and military plausibility of making the shift from offense dominance to defense dominance were to become clearcut, it would not be easy to make so radical a change in the strategic relationship and accept the denial of one's deterrent. It is not at all clear *how* to get from here (offense dominance) to there (defense dominance).

Realistically, then, the preconditions for moving toward the President's vision of a dominant defense extend beyond presently unforeseeable technical and operational breakthroughs, and require a framework of effective restraints on offensive forces. Also required would be prior agreement on ABM systems to be deployed, and an underlying deep mutual respect and trust which some desire but few anticipate soon. Even then, agreement on ABM deployments would not be easily reached, because of the inherent ambiguity of "defense" and the complications that would be introduced into the preservation of confidence in offensive limitations (especially if sharply reduced levels had been achieved, with heightened sensitivity to small perturbations or miscalculations). Deployment of ABM would involve other stresses on the strategic balance—the heightened threat which their inherent ASAT capability would constitute for satellite warning and communications systems, for example.

When the costs for a multi-layered nationwide ABM defense system are factored in along with the ambiguities and instabilities of introducing ABM even after a broad arms control regime has been put in place for strategic offensive arms, it is far from clear that the shift to ABM would be judged reassuring and stabilizing, or worth the cost. It will remain an intriguing possibility for the uncertain future, but a possibility rather than a clearly desirable goal.

The SDI: Allies and Third Countries

In NATO Europe President Reagan's March 23 speech and the reoriented U.S. ABM program have been received cautiously, with skepticism predominating. European officials and defense experts have, since the late 1960s, followed the development of U.S. and Soviet ABM programs, the SALT I negotiations, and the debate as to the impact of ABM on strategic stability. The ABM Treaty has come to be regarded as one of the few remaining cornerstones both of arms control and of U.S.-Soviet strategic stability. There is also technical skepticism that even the most exotic technology can shift the advantage drastically from the offense to the defense. American interest in such systems can be deprecated as another instance of American fascination with technical military solutions for problems which Europeans tend to see as fundamentally grounded in political differences requiring political solutions.

Europeans are by no means indifferent to reported Soviet ABM development programs or willing to leave the field to the Soviets. In October 1983, the North Atlantic Assembly (composed of NATO parliamentarians) endorsed continued U.S. ABM research programs:

> However undesirable some feel an American ballistic missile defense system would be, the presence of solely a Soviet system would be still less desirable. Thus, while Soviet missile defense research continues, there is every reason for American research to continue also . . . the Atlantic alliance should not fall behind in these areas of research in order to negotiate from a position of strength and—if necessary—to match future Soviet deployment of ballistic missile defense systems.[110]

[110] As quoted in Michael Feazel, "Europeans Support U.S. Space-Based Systems," *AWST*, October 24, 1983, p. 59.

The parliamentarians asked, however, that priority be given to negotiating verifiable arms control.

If new technology were to develop in a way making strategic ABM more feasible for the United States, it is not clear how European attitudes would be affected even given U.S. willingness to seek to extend ABM coverage to allies. The geographic position of Europe means that flight time for Soviet ballistic missiles is a third to a half that for intercontinental missiles. Given the diversity of other Soviet nuclear delivery systems, including short-range missiles and other battlefield weapons, the Soviet Union does not appear to lack means of nuclear attack on Western Europe even if its ICBMs and SS-20s were to be countered and rendered at least partially ineffective as a result of ABM deployment. The conditions of ABM engagement against ballistic missiles—in particular the very short times[111]—and the apparent necessity for automatic U.S. ABM response to a perceived attack would remove the European political authorities even further and more obviously from any role in decisions as to nuclear war. Developing a European ABM system, even if the U.S. would cooperate fully and make its technology available, appears very costly, with dubious effectiveness.

In the current framework of mutual deterrence, U.S. strategic nuclear forces provide the major element of nuclear deterrence for NATO Europe. They play a key role in the NATO strategy of "flexible response" designed also to deter Soviet conventional attack by evoking the spectre of nuclear conflict if such an attack should be launched and appear to be succeeding. What considerations would influence how an effective U.S. ABM defense system would be viewed in Europe from this perspective?

Ever since the United States became vulnerable to Soviet missile strikes, Europeans have been troubled about the American nuclear guarantee. In a crisis, would the United States really use its nuclear weapons against the Soviet Union in the face of likely Soviet retaliation against American cities—and would the Soviet Union believe the United States would initiate such a mutually destructive exchange? The current U.S. deployment of GLCM and Pershing-II missiles in Western Europe is in large part one way of trying to ease these European doubts about U.S. recourse to its intercontinental strategic forces for defense of Europe.

If the United States were to deploy a more or less "leakproof" ABM defense system for the U.S., Europeans might still not be reassured, even if the Soviet Union were only able to field one much less effective. The United States might then be more willing to resort to first use of nuclear

---

[111] The slower reentry speeds of intermediate-range missiles (such as the SS-20) would facilitate terminal defense of hard targets, but would not help much for defense of cities.

75

weapons against the Soviet Union. But an absence of Soviet response is inconceivable, and if the United States were indeed a "sanctuary," the surrogate target for the Soviets could well be NATO Europe and U.S. and other NATO forces there. The countries of NATO Europe would thus become nuclear hostages to the Soviet Union in a new and more frightening sense, since they would become the preferred and only target of retaliation to a U.S. blow against the Soviet Union which again would be decided without their having a veto or perhaps even a voice.

Such scenarios may appear arbitrary and far-fetched; they represent the kind of nuclear contingencies, however, from which NATO force planning and military strategy proceed. The dilemmas are insoluble. In the face of them, NATO Europeans have usually felt more comfortable with a situation in which the United States as well as Western Europe is vulnerable in the event of nuclear war—on the strategic rationale that so long as the Soviet Union is also vulnerable nuclear war is unlikely, but also on the human sentiment that in an alliance the members ought to share similar risks.

If the Soviet Union also deploys an effective ABM defense, the calculation is different. The Soviet Union would presumably then find it easier to reach a decision to attack NATO Europe conventionally since it could protect itself against nuclear attack and ignore the U.S. nuclear guarantee to Europe. In effect the U.S. strategic forces would be decoupled from the defense of Western Europe. If the United States did use theatre nuclear weapons to stop attacking Soviet forces in Europe, NATO Europe would find its worst nightmare coming true—Central Europe would be a nuclear battleground from which the two superpowers stood aloof. More complex scenarios can be envisaged, involving reliance on forces such as French and U.K. SLBMs and the U.S. Euromissiles to threaten the Soviet homeland and thus deter the Soviet Union; but they are so disproportionately small and uncertain as a deterrent that they have never appeared plausible alone as a substitute for the U.S. deterrent.

The prospect of revival of ABM deployments thus brings Western Europe not reassurance, but uncertainties and perhaps greater dangers should it come about. In the short term, American interest in ABM exacerbates other concerns—the American confrontational approach to the Soviet Union, an arms buildup which many see as seeking military superiority and a nuclear war fighting capacity, and a readiness to use military power and a scorn for negotiations and political processes. Appropriate U.S. and Soviet actions (as distinct from speeches) to resume serious dialogue, to bargain out mutually beneficial arms control agreements instead of maneuvering for propaganda advantage while weapons programs go ahead, and to resolve other differences where vital interests are not at stake could help remove or reduce such suspicions. They would still leave a predisposition in Europe to believe it would be better for neither superpower to pursue ABM deployments than for either or both to resume them, as well as skepticism that any security gain can accrue to either side at all proportionate to the costs and tensions.[112]

The United Kingdom and France, as independent nuclear powers with small but militarily significant deterrent forces, have a special perspective. The ABM Treaty validated and simplified their position. Deployment of a substantial, let alone a leakproof, Soviet ABM defense would put their position in doubt, at least in domestic politics. The planned modernization of both forces, with a marked increase in the number and penetrating efficiency of warheads, might in fact leave them with a minimum but real deterrent against any but a fully leakproof Soviet ABM. Even the presently planned deployments are expensive and subject to political challenge, however. Emergence of a new Soviet ABM program would reopen debate among defense experts as well as politicians, call for some response and added expense, and complicate the task of defining a plausible nuclear strategy and getting public support for it. Even more clearly than for the rest of NATO, then, the status quo on ABM is preferable.

The effectiveness of French and U.K. strategic deterrent forces is not of interest only to them, however. Even though of vastly smaller scale than the strategic forces of the superpowers, they weigh in the strategic balance and contribute to NATO's deterrent forces. This is explicitly recognized in the "Declaration on Atlantic Relations," signed by NATO Heads of Government in Brussels on June 26, 1974:

> The European members who provide three quarters of the conventional strength of the Alliance in Europe, and *two of whom possess nuclear forces capable of playing a deterrent role of their own contributing to the overall strengthening of the deterrence of the Alliance*, undertake to make the necessary contribution to maintain the common defence at a level capable of deterring and if necessary

---

[112] The *New York Times* reports that the government of FRG Chancellor Kohl is growing increasingly concerned about the implications of the Reagan Administration's proposals to develop antisatellite weapons and antimissile defenses. Officials in Bonn are reported as saying they fear the proposals could start a new arms race and strategically divide the United States from its European allies. Defense Minister Manfred Woerner is quoted as saying, "One cannot say anything against the research efforts. My concerns would begin when the West under certain circumstances or the Americans would begin building such systems, because in the final analysis I think this would not lead to stability, but just the opposite." He reportedly expressed to Secretary Weinberger concern that the development of an American antimissile defense could lead to a "Fortress America" mentality in the United States. West German military experts are cited as believing that an effective antimissile defense is extremely improbable—and even less likely if the system must defend against medium-range and tactical missiles fired in Europe. See James M. Markham, "Bonn Is Worried by U.S. Arms Research," *New York Times*, April 14, 1984, p. 3.

repelling all actions directed against the independence and territorial integrity of the members of the Alliance . . . [emphasis supplied].[113]

In Japan, strategic nuclear issues have been less intensively debated than in NATO Europe. Japan too is interested in the U.S. "nuclear umbrella" but less searching in examining just how it becomes more or less effective. There is not the same "coupling" between conventional defense and nuclear deterrence. Provided U.S. strategic, air, and naval power appears in balance with Soviet power, the refinements of deterrence theory are not pursued. Since maintaining a solid U.S. balance offsetting Soviet power is increasingly supported by Japanese leaders and the public, U.S. programs to insure that the Soviet Union does not quickly seize a lead in strategic defense can expect Japanese understanding. But the Japanese do not feel comfortable with the nuclear arms race, and avoiding its extension into space and a revival of ABM would be, by far, preferred. There is a good deal of skepticism about the prospects for arms control among Japanese leaders, but a strong insistence that efforts toward arms control be kept up. And, like the West Europeans, they are neighbors of the Soviet Union, must coexist with it and would like to do so at peace, and are wary of American actions which appear to step up the arms race and military confrontation and downplay efforts to ease political tensions. Thus initial Japanese reactions to the March 23 speech and to subsequent U.S. debate (summarized in Appendix E) express skepticism on the scientific feasibility and concern that a new form of the arms race may appear.

China has not publicly related to her own security interest the ongoing superpower ABM research and development programs, nor the new long-term U.S. interest in developing new technology to alter the offense-defense strategic equation (see Appendix E). The lively discussion in Chinese publications repeats familiar themes in the American public debate, and may indicate indirectly that these matters do draw some attention from Chinese political and military leaders. Rather than pointing out the virtues of the ABM Treaty for strategic stability and for the effectiveness of China's minimum deterrent, Chinese commentators point to the reverse factors—the impact of ABM development on the U.S.-Soviet arms race, the additional impulse that any U.S. intent to recapture strategic superiority would give to the arms race, the possibility of violation of arms control treaties, and the net increased risk of nuclear war.

With their customary realism—and without the French and British problems of public opinion and budget justifications for their strategic programs—the Chinese may well have concluded that, whatever the eventual long-term impact of ABM progress on their deterrent posture, their

---

[113] *The NATO Handbook* (Brussels: NATO Information Service, February 1976), p. 76.

78

geographic situation enables even their present small strategic forces to have some weight against any Soviet inclinations to nuclear action or blackmail. Any Soviet ABM breakout will not change that situation overnight. In the meanwhile, their public posture of implicit support for arms control and an end to the U.S.-Soviet arms race in ABM as well as other areas puts them on the side of the world majority at no cost to China.

Would U.S. (and perhaps further Soviet) ABM deployment serve to discourage proliferation of nuclear weapons capabilities to additional nth countries? The disincentive is not easy to see. Potential nth countries are motivated to undertake nuclear weapons programs to deter or threaten their regional neighbors, or to establish their status as important nations regionally or globally. Attacking the U.S. or the Soviet Union—against which ABM would defend—is low if anywhere on the list of reasons; indeed, the possibility that a superpower might find its interests sufficiently threatened to act to snuff out an incipient nuclear program is more likely to be a restraining consideration. Thus, a U.S. ABM program would have no direct influence against the nuclear ambitions of the countries presently on the list of potential nuclear weapon states.

Enhancing Stability and Arms Control Prospects under ABM Limitations

The preceding analysis highlights the uncertain prospects for development of an effective ABM system. Despite formidable advances in technology and prospects for further progress, severe operational problems remain. In the face of the destructive power of nuclear warheads delivered by ballistic missiles, it is still highly doubtful that any foreseeable technology can change the offense-defense equation to favor the defense. More sobering is the concern that deterrence will be undermined, and with it the modest degree of strategic stability now existing, if pursuit of ABM is intensified toward a presidentially stated goal at odds with the agreed premises and purposes of the ABM Treaty.

If the ABM route is a dubious one, must we pursue it as our only hope, or are there alternatives which offer more promise at less risk?

Fortunately, there are such alternatives and mutually supporting options—though each of them would be threatened by unrestrained ABM development and deployment. These alternatives proceed from the premises on which both U.S. strategic planning and complementary U.S. strategic arms control efforts have rested over recent decades, as currently reflected in the report of the Scowcroft Commission.

Chances of nuclear war are reduced if deterrent forces are *survivable* rather than vulnerable; are *not attractive* targets because an attacker would have to expend more warheads and other effort in destroying targets than they are worth; and can *penetrate* without fear of failure if retaliation were to be necessary. One route to enhance U.S. deterrence in our strategic posture is set forth in the Scowcroft Commission report, which was endorsed by the President in April 1983. It recommended, in effect:

- to maintain and improve the survivability of deterrent retaliatory forces, individually and through the synergy of the characteristics of the diverse components which assures that the majority of warheads will survive under any attack scenario;
- to reduce the value and attractiveness of vulnerable targets such as MIRVd ICBMs or large Trident submarines by replacing them in due course with individual units of lower value such as Midgetman and smaller submarines; and
- to assure the penetration effectiveness of the retaliatory missiles.

The last goal is partly to be achieved by unilateral measures such as diversified forces and penetration aids. It is also made substantially easier by the ABM Treaty, which for twelve years has guaranteed the penetration of missiles by drastically limiting ABM defenses. It is the prime example of how arms control can complement and reinforce national strategic policies and programs. If progress is made in ensuring the survivability of retaliatory forces and in reducing the value and attractiveness of vulnerable targets, it will become easier for each side to accept the penetration capability of the other's offensive missiles. If such progress is not made, ABM will continue to be considered to the extent that technical and cost factors allow.

Thus any prospects for improved effectiveness of U.S. ABM must be assessed not only in isolation but in comparison with the costs, benefits, and risks of alternative approaches. Note here that ABMs would add primarily to the deterrent value of our ICBMs by protecting them; whereas the ABM Treaty, by assuring penetration, adds to the deterrent value not only of our ICBMs but also of our SLBMs, the most survivable component of our strategic triad and the one with the largest portion of our retaliatory warheads. SLBMs at present face no significant defensive barrier to execution of their mission. Assessing deployment of an effective but partial ABM defense must weigh not only the hope of reducing the threat to survivability of our ICBMs (and to some extent our bombers) but also and probably most importantly, the cost we would pay through lessening the deterrent value of our SLBMs and surviving ICBMs as the Soviet ABM system expands in response.

Arms Control

Some proponents, as well as opponents, of ABM utilizing novel technology have acknowledged that, without limitations on opposing offensive forces, the offense is well positioned to expand or take other countermeasures to remain in a position to defeat the defense at lower cost. For space-based components, this disadvantage is compounded by the vulnerability of such components to ASAT attack.

Offensive limitations thus appear necessary for the feasibility of ABM systems, as well as for their broader purposes. Would deploying, or threatening to deploy, a U.S. ABM capability encourage or bring pressure on the Soviets to agree to significant strategic arms reduction of the sort proposed by the U.S. in the START talks?

Administration spokesmen assert that one purpose of accelerated ABM activities is to bring additional pressures on the Soviets to negotiate seriously. The rationale has not been articulated beyond generalities, though it is frequently asserted and widely accepted that:

> U.S. work on ballistic missile defense technology in the 1960s and early 1970s appears to have been an important factor in Soviet willingness to agree to the deployment limits imposed by the ABM Treaty; similar considerations can be expected to play a role in future Soviet decisions on the deployment of ballistic missile defenses.[114]

That history, however, is relevant to prospects for further negotiations to maintain or extend the scope of the ABM Treaty; as such, it will be discussed below.

The more general rationale for pursuing ABM seems to be that the Soviets are driving the offensive strategic arms race by their unremitting buildup and their alleged aspiration to obtain strategic superiority and utilize it at least for political pressure on U.S. allies and the United States. It is argued that, if they see that this effort is doomed to frustration by present U.S. strategic programs, reinforced perhaps by major ABM development, they will abandon their dangerous ambitions and bargain seriously for reductions focused on their threatening and destabilizing ICBMs. This appears to be the thrust of the following excerpt from a recent speech by Dr. George A. Keyworth, Science Advisor to the President:

> Now Soviet leaders are pragmatic—and smart. When confronted with mounting evidence that they're facing a future in which the ICBM will lose its previously unchallenged position as a devastating first-strike weapon, they'll shift their strategic resources to other weapons systems. *They'll* change *their* perception of strategic war. Critics cite this as a failing, but I see it as a major plus. If we can reduce the effectiveness of the ICBM, we can make it far easier to negotiate its reduction and elimination. *Let* the Soviets move to alternate weapons systems, to submarines, cruise missiles, advanced technology aircraft. Even the critics of the President's defense initiative agree that *those* weapons systems are far more stable deterrents than are ICBMs . . . if *we* can be the first

---

[114] *Defense Against Ballistic Missiles: An Assessment of Technologies and Policy Implications*, op. cit., p. 8.

to develop defensive deterrent capabilities, we would have a persuasive negotiating posture for arms reductions. We could then approach the Soviets with the mutual knowledge that their immense ICBM fleet no longer has the intimidating effect it once had. Under those circumstances, we could propose to join them in methodically eliminating the ICBM as the premier weapon of strategic war.[115]

So far, the evidence seems to be that the pressure of U.S. strategic modernization has been counterproductive for arms control. The number of warheads is growing, and since the President's speech, the Soviets have broken off indefinitely both Euromissile and START negotiations, rather than moving toward accommodation on what we consider sound lines.

There are undoubtedly tactical and political considerations behind their actions. There is good reason also to take seriously the Soviet statement of December 8, 1983, at the adjournment of START talks, that the Soviet side feels compelled "to reexamine all the issues"[116] which are the subject of discussion at the talks. That the Soviet Union sees space-based ABM programs in this larger framework is evident, for example, in a December 21 Moscow broadcast which links revived U.S. interest in ABMs with the U.S. nuclear rearmament and production and deployment of Euromissiles, MX, Trident II, and various other cruise missiles as part of an overall nuclear strategy looking to a first or disarming strike.[117] Such broadcasts are made for propaganda effect, but the line of thinking which they reflect is grounded in agreed principles of strategic balance at SALT I, as articulated in the carefully drafted Andropov statement of March 27, 1983 (Appendix B), on the President's March 23 speech.

Thus it would be logical for the Soviets to be reexamining, in the light of prospective presidentially sponsored U.S. ABM deployments, the START proposals of both sides. The Soviet proposal envisages a 25 percent reduction in overall strategic delivery systems totals and continuing restraints on MIRVs. The U.S. position concentrates on MIRV and throwweight reductions, and possible subsequent movement away from large MIRVd missiles to smaller single-warhead missiles. If the Soviets must be prepared to cope with a U.S. ABM deployment, and counter and penetrate it, how will deep cuts in retaliatory delivery systems and warheads, and a move away from MIRVs to single warheads, look to them? This has been an issue for the U.S. too. One justification for the MX missile advanced by the Scowcroft Commission relates to the ABM Treaty: "it is important to be able to match any possible Soviet breakout from that

[115] Keyworth, op. cit., pp. 18-19 [emphasis in the original].
[116] Frank Prial, "Soviets Won't Set a Date for Resumption of Strategic Talks," *New York Times*, December 9, 1983, p. 16.
[117] See "U.S. Missile Development Plans Viewed," *FBIS*, vol. 3, no. 250, December 28, 1983, USSR International Affairs, pp. AA 1-2.

treaty with strategic forces that have the throwweight to carry sufficient numbers of decoys and other penetration aids; these may be necessary in order to penetrate the Soviet defenses which such a breakout could provide before other compensating steps could be taken."[118] Will the Soviets feel any differently about the value of just those heavy MIRVd missiles they now have which we wish them to reduce or give up? Soviet scientists may be skeptical about the feasibility of the more exotic ABM technology, but Soviet leaders have considerable respect for American science and industry and a conservative approach to defining their strategic requirements.

Thus it is easier to see how the U.S. ABM program and the President's firm commitment to ABM goals will complicate START negotiations, than how it will give them new and healthy impetus. Behind the negotiations, in the strategic programs of the two sides, the familiar process of technology and program commitments outstripping arms control planning and agreement will march ahead. The increase in U.S. ABM research and development programs will be matched by Soviet acceleration. Charges of non-compliance with the ABM Treaty will increase (Soviet and U.S. mobile radars; ATM development programs and even deployments with potential or actual ABM capabilities; additional Soviet radar deployments and U.S. development of optical airborne sensors serving ABM radar functions). These will heighten suspicions and tension and be used to justify the offsetting programs of the other side; they will complicate resolution of verification difficulties if not dealt with in the SCC openly and cooperatively.

The SALT I negotiating history recognized the interaction between strategic defensive and offensive systems, explicitly cited in the preambles to both the ABM Treaty and the Interim Offensive Agreement. Development and deployment of ABMs puts added pressure on an opponent to improve, diversify, and multiply offensive delivery systems and warheads in order to maintain deterrence through the ability to overwhelm or evade the ABM defensive shield. This reactive phenomenon was evident in U.S. strategic planning of the 1960s prior to SALT I. In particular, U.S. development and deployment of MIRVs on ICBMs and SLBMs were originally motivated and justified primarily by the need to cope with observed Soviet ABM development activities, and initiation of deployments around Moscow.

So much for the effect of a new U.S. ABM program on Soviet programs and Soviet attitudes and positions in arms control negotiations. On the U.S. side also, one has to wonder how long serious commitment to deep START reductions, or to shifting away from large MIRVd missiles to single warhead missiles, will survive in Defense Department and congres-

[118] *Report of the President's Commission on Strategic Forces*, April 6, 1983, p. 17.

sional circles already suspicious of the Soviet Union's ABM ambitions, as added impetus appears, or is suspected in Soviet ABM preparations.

This is of course the pattern of U.S.-Soviet relations before SALT I and the ABM Treaty. The ABM Treaty in particular was a path-breaking measure to break the old cycles of unconstrained development activities, interactive weapons deployments, and suspicion and fears as to the motives of these activities and as to likely actions of the rival in times of crisis. Escape from that pattern has been halting and partial at best, as the MIRV experience shows. Measures now need to be taken to avoid reversion completely to the old pattern.

The broader questions of what motivates the Soviet Union to negotiate seriously on arms control, and of the effect of explicit U.S. pressure, cannot be answered definitively. In the case of the ABM Treaty, the U.S. Safeguard ABM program was justified to Congress and the public as a bargaining chip and as pressure on the Soviets. Yet the Soviets could equally well observe at the time that the program was in deep congressional trouble and might die of its own accord. What may have motivated them to agree to drastic ABM limits was the combination of the perception of the immaturity of their own Galosh system, the awareness of the superior American ABM technology and momentum if agreement was not reached, and the U.S. readiness to negotiate flexibly for ABM limitations meeting Soviet as well as American security criteria.

There are other precedents at hand. The effort to use prospective Pershing II and GLCM deployments to drive the Soviets off positions to which they attach great importance (the strategic character of forward based U.S. missile systems reaching the Soviet Union; the relevance of French and U.K. strategic forces) is instructive. The Soviets show an inclination to stiffen when they think that they are being pressured and their stated concerns ignored—as is understandable in human as well as great power terms.

U.S. ABM R&D will go ahead at some substantial level. That in itself should provide adequate indication to the Soviets that they cannot expect to gain advantage by refusing to hold to ABM Treaty constraints or to negotiate appropriate updating of its provisions. But U.S. unilateral movement toward a presidentially stated goal of deployment is at least as likely to have adverse effects on their readiness to bargain. And it will have other effects, of which the major one will be to give impetus not only to Soviet ABM programs but to offsetting offensive programs (penetration aids and delivery systems) which will take on their own momentum and become embedded in the strategic programs of the two sides as well as more resistant to limitation at low levels. Not everyone will view with the same complacency as Dr. Keyworth the prospects of a Soviet surge in cruise missile, advanced bomber, and submarine technology and deployments, either as making the U.S. more secure or as auguring well for deep cuts in strategic weapons.

It is impossible to say whether ABM exploiting standard or novel technology could add to stability and mutual confidence in an ultimate START regime of low levels of offensive systems. Since it appears clear that ABM defense of broad scope can work only if offensive reactions are constrained by agreement, the sensible procedure is to give priority to reducing offensive systems by measures which enhance stability as well as enforce lower levels. ABM would be introduced only by agreement in a later stage if it then appears warranted, not destabilizing, and worth the cost.

Maintaining the Viability of the ABM Treaty

Too much is at stake in the present tense state of U.S.-Soviet military and political relations to make it prudent to undermine remaining elements of stability and common understanding before we have something in which we can have more confidence as a replacement. Deterrence (as distinct from strategic superiority and its use as a threatening instrument of political and military policy) has been basic to stability and avoidance of nuclear war to date. An essential guarantee of deterrence, as recognized and defined in the ABM Treaty, has been reciprocal limitation of ABM defenses. Gradual erosion of the Treaty could imperil deterrence and heighten the risk of nuclear war more quickly than development and deployment of ABM could restore the balance. The role of the Treaty therefore needs to be understood and supported, by positive rather than merely passive adherence.

The ABM Treaty is now in its twelfth year. It has survived two formal five-year reviews. The first, in 1977, reached an unequivocal joint endorsement from the parties. The second, in 1982, produced a brief, grudging statement of continued acceptability. The next is scheduled for 1987.

U.S.-Soviet relations overall, and arms control in particular, have not evolved as was anticipated when the Treaty was signed at the Moscow Summit in 1972. We have not achieved the comprehensive limitations on strategic offensive arms, to be followed by reductions and an end to the strategic arms race, which the ABM Treaty was designed to facilitate. SALT II limitations and initial reductions were indeed negotiated, but the SALT II Treaty and associated agreements were not ratified by the United States. As of 1984, the more ambitious START negotiations designed to move directly to substantial reductions are in indefinite recess with an uncertain future, and the complementary negotiations on intermediate-range missiles in Europe are at an impasse.

Few have sought to fix the blame for this situation on the ABM Treaty, which was in fact designed to facilitate the limitation and reduction of strategic offensive arms. It was one of the foundations of the abortive SALT II agreements. Similarly, adherence to the ABM Treaty is a precondition of the de facto continuing reciprocal acceptance of the basic SALT limits on launchers and warhead fractionation and force modernization without which START will face even more formidable obstacles. The United States, which warned formally in 1972 that failure to reach more complete limitations on strategic offensive arms within five years would constitute a basis for withdrawal from the Treaty, has never seriously considered doing so. If competitive ABM deployments rather than the Treaty limits had been a feature of U.S.-Soviet strategic relations over the past twelve years, the pace of modernization, diversification, and growth of strategic offensive arsenals on each side could well have been much more rapid, rather than remaining as it did within some bounds. More basically, a resumption of preparations for large-scale ABM deployment as U.S.-Soviet overall relations worsened over the past decade could easily have heightened suspicions and tensions, and fostered mutual fears of a first strike, accompanied by reciprocal temptations to anticipate one. Such a state of crisis instability would increase chances of use of nuclear weapons by accident, miscalculation, or loss of responsible control.

Thus, the ABM Treaty is not merely a symbol of arms control hopes. As one of the few instruments by which the superpowers record their determination to avoid nuclear war and take significant action to that end, it has validated its main premise and purpose—even if precariously so.

The future of the Treaty is indeed precarious in 1984. The mutual suspicions of the superpowers in the current Cold War atmosphere extend explicitly to questioning the good faith of expressions of desire to avoid nuclear war and maintain peaceful coexistence. Each finds evidence of pursuit of strategic superiority or of preparation for a first strike in the strategic modernization and deployment plans and programs of the other. Each is eyed suspiciously by the other as preparing to break out of the Treaty deployment restraints for ominous purposes.

ABM technology has not stood still. Both nations have continued active R&D programs, professedly within Treaty provisions, but with ambiguities on each side. Computer and radar sophistication—both crucial to the efficiency of detection, discrimination, and attack of incoming warheads—have advanced markedly. So has the ability to produce and transmit high energy beams of directed energy travelling at or near the velocity of light. Mobile and airborne sensors have appeared in at least early stages of development, and some radars assertedly being built for non-ABM roles have characteristics of power, location, and configuration raising serious questions as to their conformity with Treaty provisions (Articles V and VI) limiting such developments.

The strategic situation also is changing in relevant ways. Intermediate-range and tactical nuclear missiles located in or targeted on Europe have increased in sophistication, and new types with shorter flight times to target have been deployed on both sides. The SAM upgrade issue (the potential threat to ABM Treaty limitations from enhancement of capabilities of air defense surface-to-air missiles and associated radars) with which the Treaty sought to deal under 1972 conditions has been complicated by increasing sophistication of strategic aircraft and by the beginning of deployment of cruise missiles in air-, ground-, and sea-launched modes. The SAM upgrade problem is exacerbated by improvements in air defenses designed to handle these systems. Even more challenging, the effort on both sides to develop defenses against tactical or intermediate-range ballistic missiles enhances the component and system capabilities of potential ABM systems. The new Soviet SA-12 is very much a case in point.

In these circumstances it is not enough to defend the letter of the existing Treaty or to exchange charges about compliance and suspected individual infringements. It is essential to act to keep emerging technology and its application within agreed bounds of existing Treaty provisions where possible, and of new understandings and measures where necessary. Simply challenging individual suspected violations or encroachments will produce protracted bickering, no consistent resolution of the underlying problem of maintaining the viability of the Treaty, and perhaps a situation at some point where technology and events have moved on and the Treaty is progressively a monument to past hopes. It would be ironic if this were to happen just as exploration of basic new ABM concepts and technologies now being launched convinced us that severe reciprocal restraint on ABM remains essential to strategic stability, avoidance of nuclear war, and reduction of nuclear arsenals. To let events run blindly to this end would indeed be an abdication of responsible pursuit of our national and human interests in control of nuclear arms.

Avoiding such a gradual or inadvertent undermining of the Treaty's effectiveness and agreed purpose is the positive intent of the restrictive provisions of Articles V, VI, and IX, and Agreed Statement D. These limitations on development and testing or on deployment of ABM components based on novel technology are not anti-science. They do reflect caution regarding automatic exploitation of technological advances, together with an appreciation of the sensitivity of engineering development and testing for the definition of verifiable weapons limitations. They are a joint resolution to exercise restraint and conscious choice before moving irreversibly in directions which may prove to be destabilizing.

Consultation and cooperation to take full advantage of these firebreaks deliberately built into the ABM Treaty would be the most practical and fruitful form of U.S.-Soviet cooperation on ABM technology. It would not require exchange of a good deal of sensitive technical detail on advanced sensors or kill mechanisms, or their interlinking and operations (any more than negotiation of the ABM Treaty did). By way of contrast, however, sharing SDI technology with the Soviets, which the President mentioned speculatively in a press conference following his March 23 speech, seems highly unlikely. There is no precedent, where the most sophisticated and sensitive technology is involved, and there are many barriers on both sides, at least until political relations change in a fundamental way.

Thus, to avoid once again having technological dynamics and mutual distrust dominate nuclear relations between the superpowers, the ABM Treaty as a minimum should be carefully protected while national perceptions of the future role of ABMs are being redefined and efforts are made to reinvigorate strategic arms reduction negotiations. Procedurally, this calls for utilizing fully the provisions of Article XIII on the Standing Consultative Commission. This body (which could be composed from time to time by representatives at any responsible policy level) has the charge "to promote the objectives and implementation of the provisions of this Treaty" in ways going far beyond the working out of dismantling procedures for obsolete facilities, or debating compliance issues. Especially, it is empowered to:

(d) consider possible changes in the strategic situation which have a bearing on the provision of this Treaty;

(f) consider, as appropriate, possible proposals for further increasing the viability of this Treaty, including proposals for amendments·. . .

Rather than pass over them in silence, the United States and the Soviet Union ought in the SCC to identify technological and strategic changes since 1972, and in prospect for the balance of the century, of the kind cited earlier in this Section; and try to reach agreement on whether they affect the premises of the Treaty regarding the bearing of ABM deployments or limitations on the risk of nuclear war, strategic stability, and the facilitation of arms reduction negotiations. The United States should take the initiative to explain President Reagan's March 23 vision and its implications, and to solicit and explore Soviet concerns. Verification provisions and constraints on ABM modernization ought to be examined to ascertain whether in current circumstances they require agreed clarification, interpretation, or supplement.

If ongoing research and development, and any permitted or desired limited deployments, cannot be dealt with by agreed interpretations of existing Treaty provisions, changes should by no means be excluded. They might take the form of additional protocols on the model of that in 1974, or amendment of the Treaty text if they can be negotiated. Of course any renegotiation at U.S. initiative can only be achieved if we are willing to pay a price for what we seek.

As for the U.S. ABM R&D program, its managers state repeatedly that it is being conducted scrupulously within Treaty bounds. It is no criticism of their good faith to suggest that this is not a judgment to be left to those responsible for conducting a vigorous program constantly pressing on the frontiers of technology and its exploitation. A review mechanism to insure that development activities, particularly those relating to radar and other sensors and their mobility and platforms, are indeed fully consistent, would be a valuable self-discipline. It would also place the United States in a better position for discussion with the Soviet Union of activities which should be questioned and those which should be permitted. Such an objective, nonpartisan, review panel ought to include, along with officials of the current administration, negotiators and experts from the SALT I negotiation and people of broad experience with responsibility for application of advanced technology and for U.S. strategic interests, such as those on the Scowcroft Commission.

Cooperative action could counter the corrosive effects of unilateral ABM activities which will inevitably cause disputes arising out of deliberate or unintentional divergences in interpretation of the Treaty. More important, it could reinforce confidence that the two nations see the purposes and value of the ABM Treaty in consistent ways, and that each is determined to act separately and jointly toward the fundamental aim of avoiding nuclear war.

What Should We Do?
Conclusions and Recommendations

Conclusions

Our analysis raises grave doubts, on technical and strategic grounds, that substantial acceleration or expansion of ABM research and development is warranted or prudent. Deliberation and restraint are imperative not simply because of the enormous costs of the proposed near-term SDI research and technology program, but because the strict limitation of ABM deployments is one of the few points of real agreement reached in the U.S.-Soviet dialogue about nuclear war and arms control. It has practical consequences of great importance for the effectiveness of our deterrent, for such fragile strategic stability as has been achieved, and for our prospects of avoiding nuclear war.

If defensive systems are to contribute to a safer and more stable strategic relationship between the United States and the Soviet Union, they will have to be embedded in a strict arms control regime that limits offensive systems. Technology alone will not solve the political problem of managing the strategic relationship with the Soviet Union.

The reasons for these overall conclusions will be briefly summarized, in a series of specific conclusions, and followed by some recommendations for the SDI program.

1. We do not now know how to build a strategic defense of our society that can render nuclear weapons impotent and obsolete as called for by President Reagan. Nor can one foresee the ability to achieve the President's goal against an unconstrained, responsive threat. The technical and operational considerations relevant here also raise doubts that a partially effective nationwide ABM defense will be to our net advantage, any more in the future than when the question was examined fifteen years ago.

93

On the technical side we are still at the stage of exploring basic physics, and a long-term R&D program is required to determine whether we can move to any realistic systems concepts. Each of the critical factors—the kill mechanisms; the large high quality optical systems for acquiring, pointing, tracking, and designating targets; and the battle management systems—must make enormous advances by orders of magnitude beyond anything thus far demonstrated.

Even if such technological problems are solved, there remain great operational barriers. Examples are the vulnerability of the space-based sensors and battle stations to destruction by direct attack, and the possibility of their being nullified by countermeasures available to the offense. Pop-up systems as an alternative for boost-phase intercept face severe time constraints requiring them to be based near Soviet borders and far offshore from the continental United States—contrary to Article IX of the ABM Treaty. They can be denied engagement time altogether if the offense moves to high-thrust boosters. They must be highly automated, including release authority for the weapons themselves. Furthermore, the overall multi-layered defense with its many sensors and severe battle-management requirements cannot be fully tested, but has to work perfectly in a hostile environment the first time it is turned on.

2. Intensified national programs in pursuit of ABM defenses can, and are likely to, prove destabilizing for the strategic balance and risky for our security, as each nation fears the purpose as well as the capability of its opponent's defenses.

We may view our defenses—whether largely or only partially effective—as enhancing deterrence by increasing the uncertainty of the Soviets about the potential effectiveness and success of their first strike. On the other hand, the Soviets may see (as they assert they do) our defensive program, taken together with our ongoing intensive program to modernize, diversify, and increase our offensive forces, as evidence of preparations for achieving strategic superiority and using it in a U.S. first strike: a first strike that would leave them with a weakened retaliatory force against which our defenses, though imperfect, would be relatively more effective. Of course, the same is true from the perspective of either the United States or the Soviet Union.

There is precedent for such an interaction in the history of initial ABM deployments by the Soviet Union in the 1960s which stimulated the U.S. development of MIRVs to overcome them. The evolution of Soviet MIRVs in turn led to exaggerated U.S. fears of ICBM vulnerability. Such a cycle could occur once again. The initiation of an intensified R&D program looking toward a declared ABM deployment goal is not a harmless step. Even if a deployed system never materializes, increased instability can result as both sides build up their forces to preserve their deterrent capability as well as to match each other's anticipated ABM capability.

3. Research under the SDI must be closely coupled with effective arms control progress in order to avoid the problem just described. The only prospect of an effective strategic defense depends on tightly constraining the offenses technically and numerically. Stable security cannot be achieved if only one side has defenses, or if both nations continue expanding their offenses to overwhelm each other's defenses.

But breaking out of current limitations on ABM—the principal arms control measure of major practical effect—will not enhance prospects for arms control; quite the contrary. The arms race would be given additional impetus as rival ABM development and deployments proceeded. Faced with growing ABM defenses, each side would at the same time seek to enhance the penetration capability and residual destructive power of its retaliatory ICBMs and SLBMs and their warheads. Those central missile forces would increasingly be supplemented by expanded and modernized forces (bombers and air-launched cruise missiles, other land- and sea-based cruise missiles, close-in intermediate-range ballistic missiles, and depressed trajectory SLBMs) capable of circumventing ABM defenses. In turn, enhanced air defenses with anti-cruise missile capabilities might well become imperative, with additional major expenditures.

As both sides become preoccupied with thus maintaining or exercising such options for buttressing their deterrent capabilities in the face of ABM, START negotiations would be confronted with virtually insuperable complications and obstacles to devising—let alone reaching agreement on—plausible approaches to limiting and reducing strategic offensive weapons.

4. Such an unnecessary and destabilizing acceleration of the strategic arms race, and demonstration of the futility of past arms control achievements or of future hopes, is not calculated to provide reassurance and a sense of security, in the United States or among our allies. Most of the latter have shown skepticism about the renewed U.S. interest in ABM. For themselves, close to the Soviet Union and exposed to various non- strategic as well as strategic nuclear delivery systems, hopes for effective ABM defense appear even more unlikely. If the United States does proceed with ABM deployment, more questions about the U.S. nuclear guarantee to NATO and its effectiveness would be raised than answered. Most basically, European hopes of a future of peaceful coexistence with their superpower neighbor—rather than indefinite hostile confrontation—would be again shaken by U.S. action. A U.S. ABM program going beyond research as a prudent hedge will be divisive rather than unifying in the alliance.

5. There are surer and less risky ways to enhance our deterrent while maintaining strategic stability at the same time. Stability, particularly in times of crisis, depends pivotally on the survivability of offensive deterrent forces. Ongoing programs to insure survivability for our SLBMs and a substantial portion of our intercontinental bombers—between them carrying about three-fourths of our strategic warheads—thus deserve priority attention. Terminal (hard site) ABM defense of hard military targets such as underground missile silos or command posts is another approach to survivability. It is very different from the SDI concept of defending the nation fully or partially, and is explicitly recognized in principle in the ABM Treaty, subject to careful agreed limitations. It should be debated on its merits as to feasibility and cost effectiveness. Also, strategic stability and mutual deterrence might be enhanced by moving from such attractive and threatening targets as heavily MIRVd fixed ICBMs to smaller and perhaps mobile single-warhead ICBMs, in national programs and arms control concepts.

6. In its broadest dimension, the President's March 1983 speech and the SDI now being considered challenge us to a reexamination of national purpose and ways of acting in our search for peace and security in a world where our major adversary matches us in nuclear strength and differs from us in its social and political system and in expectations as to the future course of world history. As explained in Section II, the ABM Treaty presently has a central and almost unique bearing on U.S.-Soviet relations and the prospect for cooperative pursuit of peace and security. What we do actively to enhance its constructive influence, or contrarily to undercut it deliberately or inadvertently, can have major impact on our security and the risk of nuclear war.

Reliance on mutual deterrence at the price of mutual vulnerability, which the ABM Treaty provides for, is an uncomfortable posture. It is nevertheless a realistic reaction to the situation after the advent of nuclear weapons. So long as nuclear weapons exist (even at a fraction of present numbers), deterrence through a clear common awareness of the consequences of initiating nuclear war will be prudent and indispensable. Turning to defense as an alternative is illusory. Worse, it is dangerous and destabilizing—in its failure to recognize adequately the inherent ambiguity in "defense" so long as defensive systems are combined with massive offensive arsenals, and even more fundamentally in its rejection of the basic approach to avoiding nuclear war agreed with the Soviet Union in 1972 and reflected in current strategic force postures.

Although deterrence with its accompanying threat of mutual devastation stirs profound feelings of anxiety, it is not deterrence by itself which is most disturbing for the future of U.S.-Soviet relations. It is the combination of deterrence with harsh and uncompromising confrontation—political as well as military—that is inherently ominous. The thrust of the relationship between these rival powers will have to be turned toward peaceful resolution of differences and gradual creation of conditions for peaceful coexistence, if the threatening aspect of deterrence is to be softened. To the extent mutual interests come to be identified and developed, areas of cooperation should be sought even if only warily and without excessive expectations.

Identifying mutual interests is not easy. Paradoxically, in the present situation in which nuclear competition looms large and at times dominates the U.S.-Soviet relationship, arms control and the pursuit of strategic stability have a special prominence and urgency with major political as well as strategic significance. Because the catastrophic and uncontrollable character of nuclear war is more or less clearly recognized by responsible national leaders on both sides, preventing nuclear war and shaping the strategic balance to that end with the aid of arms control has been accepted as one of the few clear areas of mutual interest even under current harsh circumstances. Arms control, however difficult, thus becomes a potential leading edge of exploratory efforts toward a more constructive political relationship between rival superpowers.

In such a context, mutual deterrence takes the form not of a simple reciprocal threat but rather of mutual self-restraint on any disposition toward initiation of use of nuclear weapons—made possible by the perception that restraint and determination to avoid nuclear war are reciprocated and concretely embodied in respective strategic forces. However grim the continuing underlying presence of nuclear arsenals makes this prospect of cooperative avoidance of nuclear war, it is superior to the vision of continued confrontation behind opposing defensive shields. The latter offers a dangerously illusory hope of safety in event of nuclear exchange, and a dangerous immediate impulse to instability and to expanded offensive as well as defensive arsenals.

7. Priority should be given to maintaining the effectiveness of the ABM Treaty as the clearest demonstration that escape from total political and strategic confrontation is possible and can have practical effect. The United States should take care not to undermine, deliberately or inadvertently, this cornerstone of efforts to move away from a future of unremitting confrontation, and thereby to enhance chances of avoiding nuclear war and of limiting and reducing nuclear arms.

Recommendations

There are concrete actions which can be taken to increase chances that the SDI program can go ahead in a way calculated to avoid destabilization.

1. The program in its size and orientation can be deliberately limited to research, for exploration of scientific possibilities and as a hedge against technological breakthroughs or Soviet ABM developments, without any commitment to subsequent development or deployment.

2. In particular, engineering development should be deliberately deferred (especially *testing* of components or subsystems whether under that name or any other such as "demonstration of capability"). This avoids not only violation of the ABM Treaty, but also a possible buildup of momentum carrying ABM technology to "points of no return," beyond which the rival power will feel it necessary to match the new capability, and beyond which confident verification (often dependent on monitoring of testing) may become increasingly difficult.

3. A SDI program so conceived need be funded at only a fraction of the $26 billion now requested for FY 1985-89—a level not very different from recent amounts is more appropriate.[119]

4. A nonpartisan advisory panel of diverse composition (with arms control and diplomatic experience going back to the 1969-72 negotiations, as well as technical expertise) might serve well in shaping and monitoring the program in this spirit. It would enhance congressional and public confidence in the purposes and prudence of the program. It would put the United States in an impeccable position for taking up quietly but firmly in the SCC cases of ambiguous Soviet activities raising questions as to their compliance with the Treaty.

5. Voluntary consultations should be initiated and regularly pursued in the SCC, at an appropriately high level of representation, under Article XIII.b and d of the ABM Treaty. The purpose would be to keep open channels of communication with the Soviet Union, our Treaty partner, as well as to maintain the viability of the Treaty in a practical sense. U.S. representatives would there make clear:

- the limited nature and purpose of our SDI research;
- our determination to comply fully with Treaty restraints (e.g., Articles V and VI and Agreed Statement D) as well as our intent to continue to raise questions about and insist on Soviet compliance;

[119] As currently proposed by the administration SDI includes, in addition to what heretofore has been identified with ABM, research on directed energy weapons and programs to enhance surveillance capabilities and the survivability of our satellites. When these programs are also included a somewhat higher funding level closer to $2 billion annually is appropriate.

98

- our readiness to explore any modifications or clarifications of the Treaty which might appear desirable in the light of post-1972 experience and technical advances in radars, interceptors, sensors, or other ABM-related technologies. In this way distinguishable boundaries might be maintained between systems or components for defenses against manned or unmanned airbreathing offensive systems or against non-strategic ballistic missiles, and those leading to ABM capabilities forbidden by the Treaty;
- our continuing appreciation of the crucial link between ABM limitations and the START negotiations on limitation of strategic offensive systems.

6. Consultations on this range of considerations, and on their own perceptions of the relation between ABM and their security, should be carried on regularly with our major allies and other countries interested in the U.S.-Soviet strategic balance.

7. In seeking to shape our own strategic programs in such a way as to enhance deterrence, increase strategic stability, and improve prospects for arms control, we should recognize that, for the foreseeable future,

- the active pursuit of partially effective U.S. strategic defense cannot be counted on to contribute to these objectives as clearly and surely as does the *absence* of significant Soviet ABMs pursuant to the ABM Treaty; and
- other strategic modernization measures (increased survivability of our deterrent forces overall; reduced ratio of warheads to missiles on these forces, especially on presently or potentially vulnerable missiles and launch systems) and related arms control measures offer more promise of timely improvement of our deterrent posture without the destabilizing consequences of renewed ABM deployment or movement toward it.

The Conclusion of President Reagan's Speech on Defense Spending and Defensive Technology[1]

Administration of Ronald Reagan, March 23, 1983

Now, thus far tonight I've shared with you my thoughts on the problems of national security we must face together. My predecessors in the Oval Office have appeared before you on other occasions to describe the threat posed by Soviet power and have proposed steps to address that threat. But since the advent of nuclear weapons, those steps have been increasingly directed toward deterrence of aggression through the promise of retaliation.

This approach to stability through offensive threat has worked. We and our allies have succeeded in preventing nuclear war for more than three decades. In recent months, however, my advisers, including in particular the Joint Chiefs of Staff, have underscored the necessity to break out of a future that relies solely on offensive retaliation for our security.

Over the course of these discussions, I've become more and more deeply convinced that the human spirit must be capable of rising above dealing with other nations and human beings by threatening their existence. Feeling this way, I believe we must thoroughly examine every opportunity for reducing tensions and for introducing greater stability into the strategic calculus on both sides.

One of the most important contributions we can make is, of course, to lower the level of all arms, and particularly nuclear arms. We're engaged right now in several negotiations with the Soviet Union to bring about a mutual reduction of weapons. I will report to you a week from tomorrow my thoughts on that score. But let me just say, I'm totally committed to this course.

If the Soviet Union will join with us in our effort to achieve major arms

[1] "Weekly Compilation of Presidential Documents," March 28, 1983, vol. 19, no. 12, pp. 423-66.

101

reduction, we will have succeeded in stabilizing the nuclear balance. Nevertheless, it will still be necessary to rely on the specter of retaliation, on mutual threat. And that's a sad commentary on the human condition. Wouldn't it be better to save lives than to avenge them? Are we not capable of demonstrating our peaceful intentions by applying all our abilities and our ingenuity to achieving a truly lasting stability? I think we are. Indeed, we must.

After careful consultation with my advisers, including the Joint Chiefs of Staff, I believe there is a way. Let me share with you a vision of the future which offers hope. It is that we embark on a program to counter the awesome Soviet missile threat with measures that are defensive. Let us turn to the very strengths in technology that spawned our great industrial base and that have given us the quality of life we enjoy today.

What if free people could live secure in the knowledge that their security did not rest upon the threat of instant U.S. retaliation to deter a Soviet attack, that we could intercept and destroy strategic ballistic missiles before they reached our own soil or that of our allies?

I know this is a formidable, technical task, one that may not be accomplished before the end of this century. Yet, current technology has attained a level of sophistication where it's reasonable for us to begin this effort. It will take years, probably decades of effort on many fronts. There will be failures and setbacks, just as there will be successes and breakthroughs. And as we proceed, we must remain constant in preserving the nuclear deterrent and maintaining a solid capability for flexible response. But isn't it worth every investment necessary to free the world from the threat of nuclear war? We know it is.

In the meantime, we will continue to pursue real reductions in nuclear arms, negotiating from a position of strength that can be ensured only by modernizing our strategic forces. At the same time, we must take steps to reduce the risk of a conventional military conflict escalating to nuclear war by improving our non-nuclear capabilities.

America does possess—now—the technologies to attain very significant improvements in the effectiveness of our conventional, non-nuclear forces. Proceeding boldly with these new technologies, we can significantly reduce any incentive that the Soviet Union may have to threaten attack against the United States or its allies.

As we pursue our goal of defensive technologies, we recognize that our allies rely upon our strategic offensive power to deter attacks against them. Their vital interests and ours are inextricably linked. Their safety and ours are one. And no change in technology can or will alter that reality. We must and shall continue to honor our commitments.

I clearly recognize that defensive systems have limitations and raise certain problems and ambiguities. If paired with offensive systems, they can be viewed as fostering an aggressive policy, and no one wants that. But with these considerations firmly in mind, I call upon the scientific community in our country, those who gave us nuclear weapons, to turn their great talents now to the cause of mankind and world peace, to give us the means of rendering these nuclear weapons impotent and obsolete.

Tonight, consistent with our obligations of the ABM treaty and recognizing the need for closer consultation with our allies, I'm taking an important first step. I am directing a comprehensive and intensive effort to define a long-term research and development program to begin to achieve our ultimate goal of eliminating the threat posed by strategic nuclear missiles. This could pave the way for arms control measures to eliminate the weapons themselves. We seek neither military superiority nor political advantage. Our only purpose—one all people share—is to search for ways to reduce the danger of nuclear war.

My fellow Americans, tonight we're launching an effort which holds the promise of changing the course of human history. There will be risks, and results take time. But I believe we can do it. As we cross this threshold, I ask for your prayers and your support.

Thank you, good night, and God bless you.

Excerpt from General Secretary Andropov's Interview on U.S. Military Policy

Pravda, March 27, 1983[2]

Question: President Reagan declared that he had devised a new, defensive conception. What does it boil down to in practice?
Answer: This is something that needs a special mention.

After discoursing to his heart's content on a Soviet military threat, President Reagan said that it was time a different approach was adopted to ensuring U.S. strategic interests and announced in this connection the commencement of development of large-scale and highly effective antiballistic missile defenses.

On the face of it, laymen may find it even attractive as the President speaks about what seem to be defensive measures. But this may seem to be so only on the face of it and only to those who are not conversant with these matters. In fact the strategic offensive forces of the United States will continue to be developed and upgraded at full tilt and along quite a definite line at that, namely that of acquiring a first nuclear strike capability. Under these conditions the intention to secure itself the possibility of destroying with the help of the AMB defenses the corresponding strategic systems of the other side, that is of rendering it unable of dealing a retaliatory strike, is a bid to disarm the Soviet Union in the face of the U.S. nuclear threat. One must see this clearly in order to appraise correctly the true purport of this "new conception."

When the USSR and the USA began discussing the problem of strategic arms, they agreed that there is an inseverable interconnection between strategic offensive and defensive weapons. And it was not by chance that the treaty on limiting strategic offensive arms was signed simultaneously between our countries in 1972.

In other words, the sides recognised the fact, and recorded this in the

---

[2] "Andropov Interviewed on U.S. Military Policy," *FBIS*, March 28, 1983, USSR International Affairs, pp. A1-A3.

above documents, that it is only mutual restraint in the field of AMB defenses that will allow progress in limiting and reducing offensive weapons, that is in checking and reversing the strategic arms race as a whole. Today, however, the United States intends to sever this interconnection. Should this conception be converted into reality, this would actually open the floodgates of a runaway race of all types of strategic arms, both offensive and defensive. Such is the real purport, the seamy side, so to say, of Washington's "defensive conception."

Statement on The President's Strategic Defense Initiative[3]

by
The Honorable Richard D. DeLauer
Under Secretary of Defense for Research and Engineering

Introduction

In a speech to the American people a year ago, President Reagan offered the hope of a world made safe from the threat of ballistic missiles. This hope is based on recent advances of technology which may offer us, for the first time in history, the opportunity to strengthen deterrence through effective defenses, rather than only through the threat of retaliation. President Reagan is determined that we explore fully this opportunity.

To guide the efforts of those working toward this important goal, the President directed an intensive analysis to define a research program to investigate the technical feasibility of an effective defense against ballistic missiles, and to assess the implications of such a program for the prevention of nuclear war, for the deterrence of aggression, and for the prospects for arms control. This study was conducted last summer, and concluded that advanced defensive technologies could offer the potential to enhance deterrence and help prevent nuclear war by reducing significantly the military utility of Soviet preemptive attacks and by undermining an aggressor's confidence of a successful attack against the United States or our allies. The study also identified a research program that will clarify future technical options for a defensive system.

Although the study acknowledged that there are uncertainties that will not be resolved until more is known about the technical characteristics of defensive systems and the possible responses of the Soviet Union to U.S.

[3] *Statement on the President's Strategic Defense Initiative*, by the Hon. Richard D. DeLauer, Under Secretary of Defense for Research and Engineering, before the subcommittee on Research and Development of the Committee on Armed Services, U.S. House of Representatives, 98th Congress, Second Session (Washington D.C.: Department of Defense, March 1, 1984).

initiatives, it concluded that a research program should be started now. We must start now because the Soviet Union has pursued advanced ballistic missile defense technology for a number of years, and has the only active ballistic missile defense system in the world. Unilateral Soviet deployment of an advanced system capable of countering Western ballistic missiles—added to their already impressive air and passive defense capabilities—would weaken deterrence and threaten the security of the United States and our allies. Thus, our research efforts will provide a necessary and vital hedge against the possibility of a one-sided deployment. In addition, our effort could provide a potentially powerful tool to moderate the development of future offensive systems and to make the world more stable and secure.

It must be understood that our program is not a system development program. No decision has been made to develop and deploy any weapons or other elements of the potential system. Our state of knowledge of the relevant technologies is inadequate. Consequently, the aim of this program is to improve our knowledge of the relevant technologies by providing firm calculations and experimental evidence on what such technologies could do, and at what cost. Put in other words, our program is a research effort to provide the evidentiary basis for an informed decision on whether and how to proceed into system development. For a full, multi-tiered system, we expect to complete the provision of this evidentiary basis by the early 1990s. A careful analysis of defensive strategy and concepts of operation is an essential element of the basis for an informed decision. Our program also includes such an analysis.

Funding

We plan an aggressive, adequately funded program to pursue the relevant technologies at the maximum reasonable rate. For fiscal year 1985 we are requesting approximately $2 billion (total for DOD and DOE). We anticipate that during the fiscal year 1986-89 period, approximately $24 billion will be required.

It is impossible to estimate now, with any precision, the full costs of developing and deploying a comprehensive strategic defense system. If a system were deployed, the ultimate costs would depend on the technological approaches selected for deployment and the size of the defensive system required. These factors, in turn, would depend in part on Soviet reactions and on the nature of future arms control agreements. It is true that the total costs would be significant in relation to our overall strategic forces program. These costs, however, would be spread over 20 years or more and could well be offset, or at least partially offset, by reduced spending on strategic offensive systems. Most importantly, costs must be judged relative to expected benefits of a system that could make nuclear war less likely.

The program is not a "new start" in the usual sense. Substantially all of the relevant technologies have been funded in previous years, but not all have been specifically related to defending against ballistic missiles. To implement the President's Strategic Defense Initiative, we have focused these previously existing related research efforts into a single program, and augmented the previously planned level of DOD funding for fiscal year 1985, $1,527 million, by $250 million, for a total request of $1,777 million. The DOD request is for 71 percent real growth in relevant technologies from fiscal year 84 to 85, and 16 percent relative to pre-SDI plans for fiscal year 1985. Part of the Initiative includes technologies involving nuclear devices, which are developed by the Department of Energy. Their work in direct support of this initiative in fiscal year 1985 is a portion of their nuclear research, development, and test funding. It is estimated at $210 million (it is not a separate, specific line item) for a total program of $2 billion.

Management

To manage the DOD's portion of this effort, we are establishing a Strategic Defense Technology Office, which will be headed by the SDI Program Manager who will report directly to the Secretary of Defense. Mr. Weinberger is presently in the process of selecting him.

The DOD portion of the program has been divided into five technical areas, and a new program element has been established for each of them. These program elements are:

1. Surveillance, acquisition, and tracking,
2. Directed energy weapons,
3. Kinetic energy weapons,
4. Systems analyses and battle management, and
5. Support programs.

These are Defense level program elements. The funds will be held in the Office of the Secretary of Defense and will be provided, at the determination of the SDI program manager, to the individual Services and Defense Agencies who will execute the individual efforts.

The Concept of Defense

The flight of a ballistic missile can be considered in four phases. The

109

first is the boost phase, in which the first and second stage rocket engines of the missile are burning. They produce an intense and unique infrared signature. In the second, or post-boost phase, the bus separates from the main engines, and the multiple warheads are deployed from the bus, along with any penetration aids such as decoys and chaff. In the third, or mid-course phase, the multiple warheads and penetration aids travel on ballistic trajectories through space, above the earth's atmosphere. In the fourth, terminal phase, the warheads and penetration aids reenter the earth's atmosphere, where they are affected by atmospheric conditions.

Our program seeks to explore technologies enabling the engagement of attacking missiles in all four phases of their flight. This would require a number of capabilities, including global, full-time surveillance to warn of an attack. There is leverage in engaging the missiles in the boost phase, because the multiple warheads and penetration aids have not yet been deployed. After deployment, we must be able to discriminate warheads from decoys, so we can target only the real threats. We must be prepared for the attacking warheads to be salvage fuzed; therefore, our terminal defenses must engage them at as high an altitude as possible. And in addition to the individual engagement capabilities, we must have a survivable battle management system capable of efficient, global control.

Included in the program are technologies for defense against the shorter range nuclear ballistic missiles, such as submarine launched ballistic missiles and theater range ballistic missiles, which may not have trajectories high enough to permit their attack with exoatmospheric systems, and which have short times-of-flight. Such technologies are important for defense of our allies.

The Technologies

Surveillance, acquisition, and tracking:

Surveillance, acquisition, tracking and kill assessment (SATKA) includes sensing of information for initiation of the defense engagement and for battle management and assessment of the status of forces before and during a defense engagement against nuclear ballistic missiles. It also includes signal processing and data processing for discrimination of threatening reentry vehicles from other objects and backgrounds. A crucial philosophy of design is that surveillance and acquisition should be autonomous in each phase of the engagement, but that tracking and kill assessment should be consultative through battle management. These requirements are necessary so that the contributions to leakage from missed detections remain independent to insure very high quality tracking and kill assessment.

The goal of this program is to develop and demonstrate the capabilities needed to detect, track, and discriminate objects in all phases of the ballistic missile trajectory. The technology developed under this program is quite complex, and any eventual system must operate reliably even in the presence of disturbances caused by nuclear weapons effects or direct enemy attack.

This program has several component technology development programs which culminate in hardware demonstrations. A focused effort to study the observables during each phase is the first major element of the program. Optical, infrared, and radar signatures of reentry vehicles and penetration aids will be measured. The new techniques of radar imaging represent another element. Similarly, optical imaging, using lasers rather than radar beams, will be pursued. Finally, a substantial effort is included to develop cooled infrared sensors and near real-time signal processing.

The technology programs outlined above will lead to a series of hardware demonstrations. Four key demonstrations have been identified at this time, with the possibility of more in the 1990s as technology progresses. One demonstration will be an advanced boost-phase detection and tracking system. Another major demonstration is designed to track and discriminate attacking objects in mid-course using advanced Long Wavelength Infrared (LWIR) sensors. The ability of airborne infrared sensors to identify and track reentering objects will be demonstrated in the Army's Airborne Optical System (AOS) development program. Ground radar imaging and tracking demonstrations will continue as part of the Army's terminal defense programs. As other technologies mature, such as radar and optical imaging, new demonstrations will be conducted. As these demonstrations are completed, we will have obtained the technical information required to decide whether defensive systems of the necessary capability can be built, considering this key element of the defense design.

Directed Energy Weapons:

This program pursues four basic concepts identified as potentially capable of meeting a responsive threat—space-based lasers, ground-based lasers, space-based particle beams, and nuclear driven directed energy weapons. It also provides for establishment of the National Tri-Service Laser Test Range at White Sands Missile Range, NM. The basic technical thrusts include beam generators (lasers and particle accelerators), beam control, large optics, and acquisition, tracking and pointing. Our request includes funds to search for technological opportunities for new and innovative capabilities.

The goal of the directed energy technology program is to bring the most promising concepts for boost and post-boost phase intercept to an equivalent technical maturity in the early 1990s. At that point we expect to be able to demonstrate a readiness for technology validation in system level demonstrations of the concepts selected to move into that phase. To achieve that goal we plan to demonstrate the feasibility of the leading candidate beam generators by the mid 1980s and their scalability to weapon performance levels in the late 1980s or early 1990s. In beam control we will demonstrate by the end of the decade a capability to control wavefront errors, maintain beam alignment within the system, compensate for atmospheric effects; and provide the components necessary to transmit and control the high intensity beams. In large optics, we plan by the 1990s to demonstrate several approaches for providing the large diameter ground and space-based optics required for most directed energy concepts and all surveillance systems employing optical and electro-optical sensors. In our acquisition, tracking and pointing efforts, we envision in-space tests that verify our capability to point with the necessary precision, to acquire and track targets of interest, and to provide early experiments in imaging and designation. Finally, we are considering integrated technology experiments to show that we can integrate the weapon subsystems with requisite efficiency. With these demonstrations completed we will have provided the basis for a decision whether we are ready to move into the more complex system level demonstrations required in the technology validation phase of R&D.

Kinetic Energy Weapons:

Kinetic energy weapons include interceptor missiles and hypervelocity gun systems. The primary roles for these weapons include (1) midcourse engagement of reentry vehicles not destroyed during boost or post-boost phases, and of post-boost vehicles that have not dispensed all of their RV's, (2) terminal (i.e., endoatmospheric) engagement of RV's not destroyed during the previous phases of their flight, (3) space platform defense against threats not vulnerable to directed energy weapons, and (4) boost-phase engagement of short time-of-flight, short range submarine launched ballistic missiles. Additional roles for these weapons include (1) boost phase intercept from space-based platforms, and (2) midcourse engagement from space-based platforms. The kinetic energy weapons will rely on nonnuclear kill mechanisms to destroy the intended target. The key technologies required to develop these weapons include (1) fire control, (2) guidance and control, (3) warheads and fuzing for guided projectiles capable of being launched by missiles or hypervelocity guns, (4) hypervelocity launchers, (5) and high performance interceptor missiles.

The goals of the kinetic energy weapons program are: (1) expansion of the technology data base to support the development of improved and advanced weapons and (2) development and flight demonstration of kinetic energy weapons which are designed to satisfy the SDI mission needs outlined above. Technology programs are planned for endoatmospheric and exoatmospheric interceptor designs, a hypervelocity launcher design, and the systems engineering and analysis required to integrate the various advanced subsystems and components into effective system constructs. Investigations will also be undertaken in novel and advanced techniques which have the potential for a high payoff in performance and/or cost effectiveness in the design of these weapons systems. Hardware development and flight test demonstration of a number of kinetic energy weapons system designs will also be undertaken as part of this program.

Systems Analyses and Battle Management:

This program has been divided into two technology projects. The Battle Management/Command, Control, and Communications Technology project will develop the technologies necessary to allow eventual implementation of a highly responsive, ultra reliable, survivable, endurable and cost effective BM/C^3 system for a low-leakage defense system. This BM/C^3 system is expected to be quite complex and must operate reliably even in the presence of disturbances caused by nuclear effects or direct enemy attacks. This program seeks to (1) develop the tools, methods, and components necessary for development of the BM/C^3 system, and (2) quantify the risk and cost of achieving such a BM/C^3 system to control the complex, multi-tiered SDI systems. The systems analyses project will provide overall SDI systems guidance to weapons, sensors, C^3, and supporting technologies. Tasks include threat analyses, mission analyses, concept formulation, system conceptual design, and subsystem requirements definition, system evaluation, and technology assessment for all levels of a multi-tiered, low-leakage system.

One of our early tasks will be to conduct a "sanity check" on the defense responsibilities allocated to the various phases of the multi-tiered system by the Defensive Technology Study. Even though we know that many of our weapons and sensor concepts will require orders of magnitude performance improvements to accomplish the President's defense objectives, we also know that effective overall system guidance will efficiently focus these technology efforts and help us avoid "gold plating" and "blind alleys."

Obviously, if such a complex defense system were deployed, it would require positive control of its operations. We have to assure that we can turn the system on when it is needed and assure that it is safe when not needed. Just as importantly, the system must not be regarded as a "paper tiger" by the Soviets if it is to serve as an effective deterrent to nuclear war.

113

Therefore, its credibility must be based on a demonstrated capability to manage the surveillance, tracking and intercept actions over the multi-tiers of this complex system. The information processing capability, specifically the development of complex software packages, necessary to associate outputs from multiple sensors, performing discrimination and designation, and "birth to death" tracking, plus kill assessment is expected to stress software development technology.

Our immediate need is for effective approaches and tools for achieving high performance processors and software, and responsive communications networks that provide high reliability and fault tolerance. Evaluation and demonstration of this complex defense system and its C^3 will largely depend upon simulation. Therefore, development of effective modeling and simulation tools will also be an early priority endeavor.

Support Programs:

This program element funds a collection of essential efforts designed to provide timely answers to a variety of critical SDI support related questions. The Defensive Technologies Study identified two areas that should receive priority attention in the SDI program.

First, for each weapon concept under consideration, we must develop the ability to scientifically predict the minimum energy that will be required, in a variety of engagement scenarios, to kill unhardened, retrofit hardened, and responsively hardened Soviet systems. These data will have a large effect on our choice of candidate system concepts. The feasibility of SDI may well hinge on the results of these efforts. The Lethality and Target Hardening project of the Support Programs effort is structured to provide these data.

Second, the ability of any deployed ballistic missile defense system to survive in the face of dedicated attack and to continue to function effectively must be established. The concepts, technologies and tactics necessary to insure continued system effectiveness will be defined and developed under the Survivability element of Support Programs. The output from this effort will be fed into all other elements of the SDI —particularly into the Systems Concepts and Analyses efforts.

Additionally, support programs will fund development of the technologies necessary for improved space logistics capabilities. These include the advanced orbital transfer vehicle capabilities that SDI will likely require. We will also evaluate the technical feasibility and cost effectiveness of using extraterrestrial materials for certain SDI applications.

Many SDI system elements (weapons, sensors, etc.) will require large amounts of electrical power. The Power and Power Conversion element of support programs will fund concept definition and technology development for multimegawatt power systems. This effort will fully exploit the technologies being developed in the joint NASA, DOE, DARPA SP-100 program. Both nuclear and non-nuclear systems and technologies will be considered.

The Department of Energy's Contribution to the SDI Program:

Although funded separately, the Department of Energy (DOE) program is integral to the overall Strategic Defense Initiative program. DOE funded efforts include concepts for nuclear driven x-ray lasers, survivability and lethality, and support subsystems. Other efforts, such as space-based neutral particle beam technology, are being performed by the DOE laboratories with DOD funds. A memorandum of understanding, to be signed by the Secretaries of Defense and Energy, will establish specific relationships between the elements of DOD and DOE engaged in planning and execution of the SDI. In accord with current policy, the DOE will have primary responsibility for nuclear source development, and the DOD for applications, target acquisition, beam control, and pointing/tracking. The DOE laboratories have unique facilities and capabilities to address many aspects of these difficult problems.

Conclusion

In summary, we believe that an effective defense against ballistic missiles could have far-reaching implications for enhanced deterrence, greater stability, and improved opportunities for arms control. Our efforts do not seek to replace proven policies for maintaining the peace, but rather to strengthen their effectiveness in the face of a growing Soviet threat. The essential objective of the Strategic Defense Initiative is to provide future options to diminish the risk of nuclear destruction and to increase overall stability.

By the end of the decade, we will have conducted a number of ground, airborne, and space experiments. The knowledge gained from these tests will help to identify those technologies that are most promising and support decisions in the early 1990s on whether and how to proceed with development of ballistic missile defenses.

Treaty Between the United States of America and the Union of Soviet Socialist Republics on the Limitation of Anti-Ballistic Missile Systems[4]

Signed at Moscow May 26, 1972
Ratification advised by U.S. Senate August 3, 1972
Ratified by U.S. President September 30, 1972
Proclaimed by U.S. President October 3, 1972
Instruments of ratification exchanged October 3, 1972
Entered into force October 3, 1972

The United States of America and the Union of Soviet Socialist Republics, hereinafter referred to as the Parties,

Proceeding from the premise that nuclear war would have devastating consequences for all mankind,

Considering that effective measures to limit anti-ballistic missile systems would be a substantial factor in curbing the race in strategic offensive arms and would lead to a decrease in the risk of outbreak of war involving nuclear weapons,

Proceeding from the premise that the limitation of anti-ballistic missile systems, as well as certain agreed measures with respect to the limitation of strategic offensive arms, would contribute to the creation of more favorable conditions for further negotiations on limiting strategic arms,

Mindful of their obligations under Article VI of the Treaty on the Non-Proliferation of Nuclear Weapons,

Declaring their intention to achieve at the earliest possible date the cessation of the nuclear arms race and to take effective measures toward reductions in strategic arms, nuclear disarmament, and general and complete disarmament,

Desiring to contribute to the relaxation of international tension and the strengthening of trust between States,

---

[4] U.S. Arms Control and Disarmament Agency, *Arms Control and Disarmament Agreements: Texts and Histories of Negotiations* (Washington D.C.: USGPO, 1980), p. 139.

Have agreed as follows:

Article I

1. Each Party undertakes to limit anti-ballistic missile (ABM) systems and to adopt other measures in accordance with the provisions of this Treaty.

2. Each Party undertakes not to deploy ABM systems for a defense of the territory of its country and not to provide a base for such a defense, and not to deploy ABM systems for defense of an individual region except as provided for in Article III of this Treaty.

Article II

1. For the purpose of this Treaty an ABM system is a system to counter strategic ballistic missiles or their elements in flight trajectory, currently consisting of:

(a) ABM interceptor missiles, which are interceptor missiles constructed and deployed for an ABM role, or of a type tested in an ABM mode;

(b) ABM launchers, which are launchers constructed and deployed for launching ABM interceptor missiles; and

(c) ABM radars, which are radars constructed and deployed for an ABM role, or of a type tested in an ABM mode.

2. The ABM system components listed in paragraph 1 of this Article include those which are:

(a) operational;
(b) under construction;
(c) undergoing testing;
(d) undergoing overhaul, repair or conversion; or
(e) mothballed.

Article III

Each Party undertakes not to deploy ABM systems or their components except that:

(a) within one ABM system deployment area having a radius of one hundred and fifty kilometers and centered on the Party's national capital, a Party may deploy: (1) no more than one hundred ABM launchers and no more than one hundred ABM interceptor missiles at launch sites, and (2) ABM radars within no more than six ABM radar complexes, the area

118

of each complex being circular and having a diameter of no more than three kilometers; and

(b) within one ABM system deployment area having a radius of one hundred and fifty kilometers and containing ICBM silo launchers, a Party may deploy: (1) no more than one hundred ABM launchers and no more than one hundred ABM interceptor missiles at launch sites, (2) two large phased-array ABM radars comparable in potential to corresponding ABM radars operational or under construction on the date of signature of the Treaty in an ABM system deployment area containing ICBM silo launchers, and (3) no more than eighteen ABM radars each having a potential less than the potential of the smaller of the above-mentioned two large phased-array ABM radars.

Article IV

The limitations provided for in Article III shall not apply to ABM systems or their components used for development or testing, and located within current or additionally agreed test ranges. Each Party may have no more than a total of fifteen ABM launchers at test ranges.

Article V

1. Each Party undertakes not to develop, test, or deploy ABM systems or components which are sea-based, air-based, space-based, or mobile land-based.

2. Each Party undertakes not to develop, test, or deploy ABM launchers for launching more than one ABM interceptor missile at a time from each launcher, not to modify deployed launchers to provide them with such a capability, not to develop, test, or deploy automatic or semi-automatic or other similar systems for rapid reload of ABM launchers.

Article VI

To enhance assurance of the effectiveness of the limitations on ABM systems and their components provided by the Treaty, each Party undertakes:

(a) not to give missiles, launchers, or radars, other than ABM interceptor missiles, ABM launchers, or ABM radars, capabilities to counter strategic ballistic missiles or their elements in flight trajectory, and not to test them in an ABM mode; and

(b) not to deploy in the future radars for early warning of strategic ballistic missile attack except at locations along the periphery of its national territory and oriented outward.

Article VII

Subject to the provisions of this Treaty, modernization and replacement of ABM systems or their components may be carried out.

Article VIII

ABM systems or their components in excess of the numbers or outside the areas specified in this Treaty, as well as ABM systems or their components prohibited by this Treaty, shall be destroyed or dismantled under agreed procedures within the shortest possible agreed period of time.

Article IX

To assure the viability and effectiveness of this Treaty, each Party undertakes not to transfer to other States, and not to deploy outside its national territory, ABM systems or their components limited by this Treaty.

Article X

Each Party undertakes not to assume any international obligations which would conflict with this Treaty.

Article XI

The Parties undertake to continue active negotiations for limitations on strategic offensive arms.

Article XII

1. For the purpose of providing assurance of compliance with the provisions of this Treaty, each Party shall use national technical means of verification at its disposal in a manner consistent with generally recognized principles of international law.

2. Each Party undertakes not to interfere with the national technical means of verification of the other Party operating in accordance with paragraph 1 of this Article.

3. Each Party undertakes not to use deliberate concealment measures which impede verification by national technical means of compliance with

the provisions of this Treaty. This obligation shall not require changes in current construction, assembly, conversion, or overhaul practices.

Article XIII

1. To promote the objectives and implementation of the provisions of this Treaty, the Parties shall establish promptly a Standing Consultative Commission, within the framework of which they will:

(a) consider questions concerning compliance with the obligations assumed and related situations which may be considered ambiguous;

(b) provide on a voluntary basis such information as either Party considers necessary to assure confidence in compliance with the obligations assumed;

(c) consider questions involving unintended interference with national technical means of verification;

(d) consider possible changes in the strategic situation which have a bearing on the provisions of this Treaty;

(e) agree upon procedures and dates for destruction or dismantling of ABM systems or their components in cases provided for by the provisions of this Treaty;

(f) consider, as appropriate, possible proposals for further increasing the viability of this Treaty; including proposals for amendments in accordance with the provisions of this Treaty;

(g) consider, as appropriate, proposals for further measures aimed at limiting strategic arms.

2. The Parties through consultation shall establish, and may amend as appropriate, Regulations for the Standing Consultative Commission governing procedures, composition and other relevant matters.

Article XIV

1. Each Party may propose amendments to this Treaty. Agreed amendments shall enter into force in accordance with the procedures governing the entry into force of this Treaty.

2. Five years after entry into force of this Treaty, and at five-year intervals thereafter, the Parties shall together conduct a review of this Treaty.

Article XV

1. This Treaty shall be of unlimited duration.

2. Each Party shall, in exercising its national sovereignty, have the right to withdraw from this Treaty if it decides that extraordinary events related to the subject matter of this Treaty have jeopardized its supreme interests. It shall give notice of its decision to the other Party six months prior to withdrawal from the Treaty. Such notice shall include a statement of the extraordinary events the notifying Party regards as having jeopardized its supreme interests.

Article XVI

1. This Treaty shall be subject to ratification in accordance with the constitutional procedures of each Party. The Treaty shall enter into force on the day of the exchange of instruments of ratification.

2. This Treaty shall be registered pursuant to Article 102 of the Charter of the United Nations.

DONE at Moscow on May 26, 1972, in two copies, each in the English and Russian languages, both texts being equally authentic.

FOR THE UNITED STATES OF AMERICA

FOR THE UNION OF SOVIET SOCIALIST REPUBLICS

President of the United States of America

General Secretary of the Central Committee of the CPSU

Agreed Statements, Common Understandings, and Unilateral Statements Regarding the Treaty Between the United States of America and the Union of Soviet Socialist Republics on the Limitation of Anti-Ballistic Missiles[5]

1. Agreed Statements

The document set forth below was agreed upon and initialed by the Heads of the Delegations on May 26, 1972 (letter designations added);

AGREED STATEMENTS REGARDING THE TREATY BETWEEN THE UNITED STATES OF AMERICA AND THE UNION OF SOVIET SOCIALIST REPUBLICS ON THE LIMITATION OF ANTI-BALLISTIC MISSILE SYSTEMS

[A]

The Parties understand that, in addition to the ABM radars which may be deployed in accordance with subparagraph (a) of Article III of the Treaty, those non-phased-array ABM radars operational on the date of signature of the Treaty within the ABM system deployment area for defense of the national capital may be retained.

[B]

The Parties understand that the potential (the product of mean emitted power in watts and antenna area in square meters) of the smaller of the two large phased-array ABM radars referred to in subparagraph (b) of Article III of the Treaty is considered for purposes of the Treaty to be three million.

[C]

The Parties understand that the center of the ABM system deployment area centered on the national capital and the center of the ABM system deployment area containing ICBM silo launchers for each Party shall be separated by no less than thirteen hundred kilometers.

[D]

In order to insure fulfillment of the obligation not to deploy ABM systems

[5] Ibid., p. 143.

123

and their components except as provided in Article III of the Treaty, the Parties agree that in the event ABM systems based on other physical principles and including components capable of substituting for ABM interceptor missiles, ABM launchers, or ABM radars are created in the future, specific limitations on such systems and their components would be subject to discussion in accordance with Article XIII and agreement in accordance with Article XIV of the Treaty.

[E]

The Parties understand that Article V of the Treaty includes obligations not to develop, test or deploy ABM interceptor missiles for the delivery by each ABM interceptor missile of more than one independently guided warhead.

[F]

The Parties agree not to deploy phased-array radars having a potential (the product of mean emitted power in watts and antenna area in square meters) exceeding three million, except as provided for in Articles III, IV, and VI of the Treaty, or except for the purposes of tracking objects in outer space or for use as national technical means of verification.

[G]

The parties understand that Article IX of the Treaty includes the obligation of the US and the USSR not to provide to other States technical descriptions or blue prints specially worked out for the construction of ABM systems and their components limited by the Treaty.

2. Common Understandings

Common understanding of the Parties on the following matters was reached during the negotiations:

A. Location of ICBM Defenses

The U.S. Delegation made the following statement on May 26, 1972:

Article III of the ABM Treaty provides for each side one ABM system deployment area centered on its national capital and one ABM system deployment area containing ICBM silo launchers. The two sides have registered agreement on the following statement: "The Parties understand that the center of the ABM system deployment area centered on the national capital and the center of the ABM system deployment area containing ICBM silo launchers for each Party shall be separated by no less than thirteen hundred kilometers." In this connection, the U.S. side notes that its ABM system deployment area for defense of ICBM silo launchers, located west of the Mississippi River, will be centered in the Grand Forks ICBM silo launcher deployment area. (See Agreed Statement [C].)

124

B. ABM Test Ranges

The U.S. Delegation made the following statement on April 26, 1972:

Article IV of the ABM Treaty provides that "the limitations provided for in Article III shall not apply to ABM systems or their components used for development or testing, and located within current or additionally agreed test ranges." We believe it would be useful to assure that there is no misunderstanding as to current ABM test ranges. It is our understanding that ABM test ranges encompass the area within which ABM components are located for test purposes. The current U.S. ABM test ranges are at White Sands, New Mexico, and at Kwajalein Atoll, and the current Soviet ABM test range is near Sary Shagan in Kazakhstan. We consider that non-phased array radars of types used for range safety or instrumentation purposes may be located outside of ABM test ranges. We interpret the reference in Article IV to "additionally agreed test ranges" to mean that ABM components will not be located at any other test ranges without prior agreement between our Governments that there will be such additional ABM test ranges.

On May 5, 1972, the Soviet Delegation stated that there was a common understanding on what ABM test ranges were, that the use of the types of non-ABM radars for range safety or instrumentation was not limited under the Treaty, that the reference in Article IV to "additionally agreed" test ranges was sufficiently clear, and that national means permitted identifying current test ranges.

C. Mobile ABM Systems

On January 29, 1972, the U.S. Delegation made the following statement:

Article V(1) of the Joint Draft Text of the ABM Treaty includes an undertaking not to develop, test, or deploy mobile land-based ABM systems and their components. On May 5, 1971, the U.S. side indicated that, in its view, a prohibition on deployment of mobile ABM systems and components would rule out the deployment of ABM launchers and radars which were not permanent fixed types. At that time, we asked for the Soviet view of this interpretation. Does the Soviet side agree with the U.S. side's interpretation put forward on May 5, 1971?

On April 13, 1972, the Soviet Delegation said there is a general common understanding on this matter.

D. Standing Consultative Commission

Ambassador Smith made the following statement on May 22, 1972:

The United States proposes that the sides agree that, with regard to initial implementation of the ABM Treaty's Article XIII on the Standing Consultative Commission (SCC) and of the consultation Articles to the Interim Agreement on offensive arms and the Accidents Agreement,* agreement establishing the SCC will be worked out

---

*See Article 7 of Agreement to Reduce the Risk of Outbreak of Nuclear War Between the United States of America and the Union of Soviet Socialist Republics, signed Sept. 30, 1971.

early in the follow-on SALT negotiations; until that is completed, the following arrangements will prevail: when SALT is in session, any consultation desired by either side under these Articles can be carried out by the two SALT Delegations; when SALT is not in session, *ad hoc* arrangements for any desired consultations under these Articles may be made through diplomatic channels.

Minister Semenov replied that, on an *ad referendum* basis, he could agree that the U.S. statement corresponded to the Soviet understanding.

E. Standstill

On May 6, 1972, Minister Semenov made the following statement:

In an effort to accommodate the wishes of the U.S. side, the Soviet Delegation is prepared to proceed on the basis that the two sides will in fact observe the obligations of both the Interim Agreement and the ABM Treaty beginning from the date of signature of these two documents.

In reply, the U.S. Delegation made the following statement on May 20, 1972:

The U.S. agrees in principle with the Soviet statement made on May 6 concerning observance of obligations beginning from date of signature but we would like to make clear our understanding that this means that, pending ratification and acceptance, neither side would take any action prohibited by the agreements after they had entered into force. This understanding would continue to apply in the absence of notification by either signatory of its intention not to proceed with ratification or approval.

The Soviet Delegation indicated agreement with the U.S. statement.

3. Unilateral Statements

The following noteworthy unilateral statements were made during the negotiations by the United States Delegation:

A. Withdrawal from the ABM Treaty

On May 9, 1972, Ambassador Smith made the following statement:

The U.S. Delegation has stressed the importance the U.S. Government attaches to achieving agreement on more complete limitations on strategic offensive arms, following agreement on an ABM Treaty and on an Interim Agreement on certain measures with respect to the limitation of strategic offensive arms. The U.S. Delegation believes that an objective of the follow-on negotiations should be to constrain and reduce on a long-term basis threats to the survivability of our respective strategic retaliatory forces. The USSR Delegation has also indicated that the objectives of SALT would remain unfulfilled without the achievement of an agreement providing for more complete limitations on strategic offensive arms. Both sides recognize that the initial agreements would be steps toward the achievement of more complete limitations on strategic arms. If an agreement providing for more complete strategic offensive arms limitations were not achieved within five years, U.S. supreme interests could be jeopardized. Should that occur, it would constitute a basis for withdrawal from the ABM Treaty. The U.S. does not wish to see such a situation occur, nor do we believe that the USSR does. It is because we wish to prevent such a situation that we emphasize the importance the U.S. Government attaches to achievement of more complete limitations on strategic offensive arms. The U.S. Executive will inform the Congress, in connection with Congressional consideration of the ABM Treaty and the Interim Agreement, of this statement of the U.S. position.

B. Tested in ABM Mode

On April 7, 1972, the U.S. Delegation made the following statement:

Article II of the Joint Text Draft uses the term "tested in an ABM mode," in defining ABM components, and Article VI includes certain obligations concerning such testing. We believe that the sides should have a common understanding of this phrase. First, we would note that the testing provisions of the ABM Treaty are intended to apply to testing which occurs after the date of signature of the Treaty, and not to any testing which may have occurred in the past. Next, we would amplify the remarks we have made on this subject during the previous Helsinki phrase by setting forth the objectives which govern the U.S. view on the subject, namely, while prohibiting testing of non-ABM components for ABM purposes: not to prevent testing of ABM components, and not to prevent testing of non-ABM components for non-ABM purposes. To clarify our interpretation of "tested in an ABM mode," we note that we would consider a launcher, missile or radar to be "tested in an ABM mode" if, for example, any of the following events occur: (1) a launcher is used to launch an ABM interceptor missile, (2) an interceptor missile is flight tested against a target vehicle which has a flight trajectory with characteristics of a strategic ballistic missile flight trajectory, or is flight tested in conjunction with the test of an ABM interceptor missile or an ABM radar at the same test range, or is flight tested to an altitude inconsistent with interception of targets against which air defenses are deployed, (3) a radar makes measurements on a cooperative target vehicle of the kind referred to in item (2) above during the reentry portion of its trajectory or makes measurements in conjunction with the test of an ABM interceptor missile or an ABM radar at the same test range. Radars used for purposes such as range safety or instrumentation would be exempt from application of these criteria.

C. No-Transfer Article of ABM Treaty

On April 18, 1972, the U.S. Delegation made the following statement:

In regard to this Article [IX], I have a brief and I believe self-explanatory statement to make. The U.S. side wishes to make clear that the provisions of this Article do not set a precedent for whatever provision may be considered for a

Treaty on Limiting Strategic Offensive Arms. The question of transfer of strategic offensive arms is a far more complex issue, which may require a different solution.

D. *No Increase in Defense of Early Warning Radars*

On July 28, 1970, the U.S. Delegation made the following statement:

Since Hen House radars [Soviet ballistic missile early warning radars] can detect and track ballistic missile warheads at great distances, they have a significant ABM potential. Accordingly, the U.S. would regard any increase in the defenses of such radars by surface-to-air missiles as inconsistent with an agreement.

Protocol to the Treaty Between the United States of America and the Union of Soviet Socialist Republics on the Limitation of Anti-Ballistic Missile Systems[6]

Signed at Moscow July 3, 1974
Ratification advised by U.S. Senate November 10, 1975
Ratified by U.S. President March 19, 1976
Instruments of ratification exchanged May 24, 1976
Proclaimed by U.S. President July 6, 1976
Entered into force May 24, 1976

The United States of America and the Union of Soviet Socialist Republics, hereinafter referred to as the Parties,

Proceeding from the Basic Principles of Relations between the United States of America and the Union of Soviet Socialist Republics signed on May 29, 1972,

Desiring to further the objectives of the Treaty between the United States of America and the Union of Soviet Socialist Republics on the Limitation of Anti-Ballistic Missile Systems signed on May 26, 1972, hereinafter referred to as the Treaty,

Reaffirming their conviction that the adoption of further measures for the limitation of strategic arms would contribute to strengthening international peace and security,

Proceeding from the premise that further limitation of anti-ballistic missile systems will create more favorable conditions for the completion of work on a permanent agreement on more complete measures for the limitation of strategic offensive arms,

Have agreed as follows:

Article I

1. Each Party shall be limited at any one time to a single area out of the two provided in Article III of the Treaty for deployment of anti-ballistic missile (ABM) systems or their components and accordingly shall not exercise its right to deploy an ABM system or its components in the second of the two ABM system deployment areas permitted by Article III of the Treaty, except as an exchange of one permitted area for the other in accordance with Article II of this Protocol.

[6] Ibid., p. 162.

2. Accordingly, except as permitted by Article II of this Protocol: the United States of America shall not deploy an ABM system or its components in the area centered on its capital, as permitted by Article III(a) of the Treaty, and the Soviet Union shall not deploy an ABM system or its components in the deployment area of intercontinental ballistic missile (ICBM) silo launchers as permitted by Article III(b) of the Treaty.

Article II

1. Each Party shall have the right to dismantle or destroy its ABM system and the components thereof in the area where they are presently deployed and to deploy an ABM system or its components in the alternative area permitted by Article III of the Treaty, provided that prior to initiation of construction, notification is given in accord with the procedure agreed to in the Standing Consultative Commission, during the year beginning October 3, 1977 and ending October 2, 1978, or during any year which commences at five year intervals thereafter, those being the years for periodic review of the Treaty, as provided in Article XIV of the Treaty. This right may be exercised only once.

2. Accordingly, in the event of such notice, the United States would have the right to dismantle or destroy the ABM system and its components in the deployment area of ICBM silo launchers and to deploy an ABM system or its components in an area centered on its capital, as permitted by Article III(a) of the Treaty, and the Soviet Union would have the right to dismantle or destroy the ABM system and its components in the area centered on its capital and to deploy an ABM system or its components in an area containing ICBM silo launchers, as permitted by Article III(b) of the Treaty.

3. Dismantling or destruction and deployment of ABM systems or their components and the notification thereof shall be carried out in accordance with Article VIII of the ABM Treaty and procedures agreed to in the Standing Consultative Commission.

Article III

The rights and obligations established by the Treaty remain in force and shall be complied with by the Parties except to the extent modified by this Protocol. In particular, the deployment of an ABM system or its components within the area selected shall remain limited by the levels and other requirements established by the Treaty.

Article IV

This Protocol shall be subject to ratification in accordance with the constitutional procedures of each Party. It shall enter into force on the day of the exchange of instruments of ratification and shall thereafter be considered an integral part of the Treaty.

DONE at Moscow on July 3, 1974, in duplicate, in the English and Russian languages, both texts being equally authentic.

For the United States of America:
RICHARD NIXON
President of the United States of America

For the Union of Soviet Socialist Republics:
L. I. BREZHNEV
General Secretary of the Central Committee of the CPSU

Allies and Friends Under a Strategic Defense Regime: The Asian Connection

John W. Lewis

While it is routinely asserted by most U.S. officials and specialists that American security policies have global implications, few investigate in any depth what those implications might be. As Americans, we can assume that an America immune to a Soviet missile attack would increase U.S. credibility in the eyes of allies and friends. Yet, seldom do we ask those whose views on credibility are most affected what they actually think. We also assume that those same friends and allies grasp the nuances of our policy pronouncements and assess our programs as we do. What follows is a brief review of what China and Japan—two Asian countries that are of great importance to the United States—have said concerning their assessments of President Reagan's speech on March 23, which called for an American strategic defense program.

China

The Chinese responded immediately and vigorously to President Ronald Reagan's speech on strategic defense and to his Executive Order to begin work on the development of an anti-ballistic missile system. Their responses, which are ongoing, have been detailed and sustained, and their appraisal of the Reagan plan and subsequent Soviet reactions may be grouped under these headings:

- the impact on the U.S.-Soviet arms race
- the U.S. intention to recapture strategic superiority
- the alleged violations of arms control treaties
- the increased possibility of nuclear war

In none of these responses has Beijing discussed the impact of any future missile defense system on China's strategic position or programs. This is not unusual for the PRC, for Chinese officials seldom acknowledge the influence of other nations on their own security or defense programs. Such silence, of course, does set the Chinese apart from the Europeans, though not, as it turns out, from the Japanese in respect to strategic defense.

Strategic Defense and the Arms Race

Since the breakup of the Moscow-Beijing alliance in the early 1960s, a recurrent theme in Chinese statements on the Soviet Union and the United States has emphasized their upward spiraling arms race. Whenever in the 1960s and 1970s the two superpowers seemed close to an arms agreement, the PRC characterized their actions as "collusion," but now routinely decries those efforts as constituting a crude disguise for further arms preparations. Thus, it is not surprising that most Chinese comments on U.S. strategic defense programs and the relevant Reagan-Andropov exchanges stress the arms race implications.

In March, the Chinese began their assessment of the Reagan speech by underlining Andropov's statement that strategic defense "would actually open the floodgates of a runaway race of all types of strategic arms" and was an attempt "to destroy the inseparable inter-relationship between strategic offensive and defensive weapons." The official Chinese news agency, Xinhua, commented that the Reagan and Andropov remarks showed that "both sides are carrying out their arms race in all fields on an even broader basis."[7]

What was new about such statements by China was the shift in emphasis to denunciations of "the second round of the arms race"—the race to control space. While acknowledging that this race "already has a history of more than twenty years [since Sputnik],"[8] Beijing quickly labeled the race for defensive space weapons as a novel and intensified phase. The creation of the U.S. Air Force Space Command and the parallel programs for anti-satellite warfare seemed to the Chinese to warrant the judgment that a major turning point, or at least "a new step forward," had been reached in the twenty-year struggle for space. This judgment was given special billing in a virtually unprecedented article on disarmament in the Central Committee's theoretical journal Hongqi (Red Flag) in May.[9]

This and other Chinese articles paid particular attention to the Soviet reactions to the emerging U.S. programs for strategic defense and concluded that Moscow and Washington are "dancing on a death rope."[10] In

[7] Xinhua, March 27, 1983.
[8] Renmin ribao, March 29, 1983.
[9] Hongqi, no. 9, 1983, p. 37.
[10] Shijie zhishi, no. 9, 1983, p. 9.

134

the end, the race would not end in supremacy of either side, Beijing concluded, for "Reagan's proposition will in no way be able to match his claims for it; namely, that it will fundamentally change the United States nuclear deterrent strategy"[11] or make the Soviet Union vulnerable in such a one-sided way.

The U.S. Goal of Strategic Superiority

Consistent with the stress on a new arms race was China's conclusion that the United States had adopted the goal of regaining strategic superiority. In mid-April, the press agency Xinhua released a story that outlined China's view of this goal.

> As a nuclear attack from one side is sure to incur nuclear retaliation from the other, both have been keeping a so-called balance of terror, with neither in a position absolutely superior to overwhelm its adversary. Under such circumstances, whoever makes a breakthrough in defensive strategic weapons will remain invincible, that is, capable of launching a nuclear strike without having to worry about reprisals. . . . This means an attempt [by the U.S.] to out race the Soviet Union to gain superiority.[12]

In a companion analysis of President Reagan's military strategy, *Renmin ribao* reviewed "certain trends" in U.S. strategic thinking and summarized them as an ever "greater loss of confidence" in deterrence, a greater flexibility to regain the strategic initiative, and "a greater use of one's own strong points to attack enemy weaknesses."[13] The key problem underlying these trends was "to find strategic ways to solve the contradiction between 'means' and 'ends.' " The article acknowledged that American technological prowess was a "strong point" in the U.S. effort to regain superiority. One PRC journal commented in May that by using modern science and technology "to turn the 'Star Wars' type of science fiction into reality," Reagan was attempting to make the U.S. invincible.[14] This means, it said, "an attempt to out race the Soviet Union to gain superiority," and it linked that effort to other American missile programs, particularly the deployments of cruise and Pershing II missiles in Europe.[15] The Chinese went on to observe that the Russians would never allow the United States to gain a decisive strategic advantage; hence, the upward spiraling arms race. After reviewing the strategic defense proposal in the light of other programs, *Guangming ribao* observed: "From the long-term point of view, the

[11] Xinhua, June 11, 1983.
[12] Xinhua, April 15, 1983.
[13] *Renmin ribao*, May 5, 1983. Earlier, a similar review of Soviet military strategy was published in *Shijie zhishi*, no. 16, 1983, pp. 5-6.
[14] *Beijing Review*, no. 18, 1983, p. 10.
[15] *Guangming ribao*, May 18, 1983.

contention for nuclear superiority [between the superpowers] will never come to an end."[16]

Violation of Arms Control Treaties

Almost immediately after the Reagan speech in March, the Chinese related U.S. plans for strategic defense to the probable violation of arms control agreements in place, and to the likely demise of any genuine arms control efforts in general. On March 29, they reported "that in spite of the Outer Space Treaty of 1967, both the United States and the Soviet Union have pursued visions of space wars."[17]

The major article on disarmament in the journal *Hongqi*, referred to above, took the U.S. move as additional evidence of Washington's disinterest in any substantial arms reductions. It said that both superpowers had this general view:

- strengthen oneself and weaken one's opponent in order to make disarmament serve the purpose of achieving military superiority
- work out some rules of the game to control the economic burden of arms expansion and war preparations
- maintain nuclear predominance over other nations and restrain and prohibit other nations from developing their own nuclear strength
- assume a pose of disarmament and negotiations in order to cope with the strong [popular] tides opposing the arms race[18]

While noting that the U.S. President had denied that research and development on a missile defense system violated any treaties, the Chinese made clear their conviction that neither superpower would pay much attention to treaty restraints in any case. *Renmin ribao* said with some scorn:

Although the two superpowers . . . signed the anti-ballistic missile treaty which stipulated that deployment and even development of a space-based military system is forbidden, both countries have spared no efforts in doing research on and developing their own space weapon systems under the cover of this treaty.[19]

The Chinese, during this period, dramatized their growing interest in disarmament by becoming a party to another arms control agreement, the Antarctica Treaty, and a member of a major international body, the International Atomic Energy Agency (IAEA). They used these occasions to restate their own interest in arms reductions and control, and to

[16] Ibid.
[17] Xinhua, March 29, 1983.
[18] *Hongqi*, no. 9, 1983, p 37.
[19] *Renmin ribao*, March 29, 1983.

contrast their interest with that of Moscow and Washington.[20] The Chinese earlier had signed the Geneva Protocol for the Prohibition of the Use in War of Asphyxiating, Poisonous or Other Gases, Protocol II of the Latin American Nuclear-Free Zone Treaty, and the Convention on Prohibitions or Restrictions on the Use of Certain Conventional Weapons. They had also joined the UN Commission on Disarmament and put forward a series of proposals on both conventional and nuclear disarmament. In respect to the IAEA membership, the head of the Chinese delegation to the Agency, Wang Shu, said:

> We respect the desire of a great many non-nuclear weapon states not to test, use, manufacture, produce, and acquire nuclear weapons. . . . China neither stands for nor encourages the proliferation of nuclear weapons.[21]

Since the early 1980s, the Chinese have contrasted their own growing commitment to the disarmament process, including the reduction of their military budget, to the failure of the superpowers to uphold even those limited arms control agreements that had been negotiated.[22]

Increased Danger of Nuclear War

The Chinese press has linked the race in the strategic defense field, the struggle for superiority, and the decline of arms control to the greater likelihood of nuclear war. Whatever Chinese Maoists might once have said about nuclear weapons being "paper tigers," the current leaders appear to have a much more realistic view of the consequences of nuclear war for themselves as well as the United States and the Soviet Union. The main conclusion is that the arms race for a strategic defense has produced "unprecedented tension whether in speed, in scale, or in the standards [of warfare]. All of their activities have aggravated international tension and are seriously imperilling world peace."[23]

As noted earlier, Beijing has downgraded the likelihood that the United States will forego the development and deployment of offensive systems while fashioning its strategic defenses. China noted that Reagan's announcement on an ABM defense system had virtually coincided with a threat to deploy Pershing II "missiles, which the Soviet Union is most worried about, in Alaska near the Soviet border."[24]

The Chinese, who had long been skeptical about European peace movements—as potentially serving Soviet purposes—turned strongly in their favor after the Reagan announcement in March:

[20] Ibid., May 10, 1983; and Xinhua, October 11, 1983.
[21] Xinhua, October 11, 1983.
[22] *Hongqi*, no. 9, 1983, pp. 37-40.
[23] *Renmin ribao*, October 11, 1983.
[24] Xinhua, April 8, 1983.

Mankind is now faced with the danger of nuclear war because of the nuclear arms race between the superpowers. Therefore, the struggle by the people of the various countries against the nuclear arms race . . . is a necessary component of the current general struggle . . . to safeguard world peace.[25]

Preventing nuclear war had become the ultimate issue of disarmament, Beijing argued, and "it is natural that all peoples throughout the world are paying close attention to it."[26] The Chinese suggested, but did not say directly, that the non-nuclear and small states had suffered the most from the arms race and would have the most to lose from a race to make the superpowers invincible.[27] *Renmin ribao* in May compared that race to the Chinese saying that "the man of Qi was haunted by fear that the sky might fall." Today, it said, that is a "real threat." "If the two superpowers do not stop the space arms race and disarm their 'celestial warriors,' people will regret that they are not as lucky as the man of Qi."[28]

Japan

Tokyo's official views of American defense programs mirror some of the concerns voiced by Beijing. Yet, they also reflect the special tensions between Japan's military dependence on the United States and its vulnerable security position in Asia. While Tokyo, like Beijing, has shown an ever greater interest in U.S.-Soviet arms control negotiations, the principal Japanese concern focuses on the importance of maintaining a U.S. counterbalance to Soviet power. In particular, Japan has watched how the negotiations on European-based intermediate-range nuclear forces would affect the buildup of the Soviet SS-20 force in East Asia.[29] Whatever the outcome of those negotiations, the current Japanese Government applauds the U.S. defense efforts which, it holds, "are strictly aimed at maintaining and strengthening the credibility of its deterrent power in response to Soviet military buildup."[30] This statement was echoed by the head of the Defense Agency, Kazuo Tanikawa, on the day President Reagan presented his concept of strategic defense: "Japan should welcome the U.S. presence in the Pacific region if its military reinforcements lead to

[25] Ibid.
[26] *Hongqi*, no. 9, 1983, p. 38.
[27] Ibid., pt. iii; see also *Renmin ribao*, May 5, 1983.
[28] *Renmin ribao*, May 19, 1983.
[29] See, for example, Japan Defense Agency, Defense of Japan, 1982, 1983 (Tokyo: Japan Times, 1982 and 1983), pt. 1, sections 2 and 3. A new section 4, p. 15, in the 1983 volume noted: "Japan strongly hopes that the INF negotiations will make progress and that SS-20s will be abolished or reduced on a global basis."
[30] Ibid., 1983, p. 10.

improving the U.S. deterrent against the Soviets."[31] The politics of defense in Japan are far more complex than this suggests, but the official position enjoys considerable national support.

In Seoul, the Koreans immediately reported on the Reagan "futuristic defense plan" and described it as a "major departure from the three-decade-old strategy of nuclear deterrence."[32] But, at least in official reports, the Japanese largely ignored the plan. Where some Korean newspapers welcomed strategic defense as a possible "new device to head off [Soviet] adventurism for nuclear war,"[33] the Japanese paid far greater attention to the "expanded version of the sea areas in which Japan's Self-Defense Forces might escort or protect American warships in the interest of Japan in case of emergency."[34] Neither Korea nor Japan considered what steps might have to be taken to defend their homelands in the event of a nuclear conflict.[35]

The initial press coverage in Japan concerning the U.S. President's strategic defense proposal reviewed the available technologies and stressed the U.S. abandonment of arms control as a means to avert nuclear war.[36] Editorial comments noted that the Reagan speech was "concerned with the promotion of the expansion of military power, as usual."[37] In general, the Japanese unofficial reactions, which were quite limited in number and duration, tended to stress these points:

- the development of defensive weapons will spread the development of weapons to a new field
- the decline of U.S. interest in arms control
- the intensification of Reagan's anti-Soviet policy

The reactions of the Japanese press to the Reagan speech were few compared to the Chinese and more general in character. They expressed

[31] *Kyodo* (Tokyo), March 23, 1983. The day before, the same news service reported that nearly six out of ten Japanese voters favored maintaining the status quo in Japan's defense capabilities.
[32] *Korea Times*, March 25, 1983. The Seoul newspaper *Choson Ilbo*, March 26, 1983, decried the Reagan plan and concluded: "The only way for human beings to survive is rational disarmament, the easing of tensions, and reconciliation, rather than such a competition [for super defensive weapons]."
[33] *Korea Herald*, March 26, 1983. It might be noted that the North Koreans confined their reactions to the Reagan plan to repeating Soviet comments. See, for example, Pyongyang Radio, March 30, 1983.
[34] *Kyodo*, March 24, 1983.
[35] Prime Minister Nakasone on April 1 called on all the nuclear powers "to make public information about [the] deployment and strength of their strategic forces [which] . . . would enable other parties to assess the substance and arguments at the INF reduction talks. . . . " See *Kyodo*, April 1, 1983.
[36] See, for example, *Mainichi Shimbun*, March 24-25, 1983.
[37] *Tokyo Shimbun*, March 25, 1983.

anxiety over the coming expansion of nuclear weapons under the guise of defense long before Reagan's vision of ending the nuclear reign of terror could be realized.

The Further Development of New Weapons

Most Japanese newspapers regard the call for strategic defense as a program to expand U.S. military power, not one to limit the arms race. The *Asahi Shimbun* in late March looked to the probable impact of the U.S. program on Moscow for clues to the outcome of strategic defense. It said:

> The Soviet Union will believe that the U.S. is equipped with the ability to launch a preemptive nuclear attack [once it has a strategic defense]. The Soviet side will either develop the attack ability to destroy the enemy's defense ability, or will try to have a similar defense ability. . . . If one side fortifies a shield, the other will sharpen a sword.[38]

This would promote a U.S.-Soviet arms race in space and would inevitably mean a struggle to perfect anti-satellite weapons.

The Decline of U.S. Interest in Arms Control

While much has been made of the two-track decision in Europe—or the belief in the complementarity of defense and arms control measures there—too little attention has been given by Washington to this belief elsewhere. The 1983 annual report of the Japan Defense Agency reiterated Tokyo's strong interest in "serious arms control negotiations between East and West,"[39] and Prime Minister Nakasone has advocated taking "a flexible but tough diplomatic posture toward the Soviet Union," as well as a closer relationship between Japan and the NATO countries in support of the U.S. position in the INF negotiations.[40] Japanese fears that the arms race would sharply accelerate were heightened in the days following the Reagan speech, when Soviet Foreign Minister Andrei Gromyko asserted the Soviet Union's "right" to deploy more nuclear missiles in Siberia to counter what he called "U.S. nuclear arms in Japan and neighboring areas."[41]

Consistent with Japan's long-standing interest in diplomatic as well as

---

[38] *Asahi Shimbun*, March 28, 1983.

[39] *Defense of Japan 1983*, p. 15. The head of the Japan Defense Agency (JDA) has said: "defense and diplomacy are two sides of the same thing, and . . . it is necessary for the Prime Minister and the JDA Director General to have a strong pipeline linking them together." See *Kankai*, March 1983.

[40] *Kyodo*, March 27, 1983.

[41] The text of the Gromyko press conference is in Moscow Radio, April 2, 1983; the main Japanese reactions can be found in *Kyodo*, April 3-4, 1983.

140

military means to deal with Soviet power, the Japanese press called for greater attention by the United States to the reduction of offensive nuclear weapons:

> if the U.S. abandons the argument for nuclear deterrence, it should head toward the mutual reduction of attack-type nuclear weapons through talks. . . . They [the superpowers] should not take steps along the road leading to the new expansion of nuclear military power, hidden by the name "defense."[42]

Another article noted that Reagan's speech contained no hint of how he intended to check the U.S.-Soviet nuclear arms race: "One cannot help but say that [Reagan's] enthusiasm for disarmament is missing."[43]

The Intensification of Reagan's Anti-Soviet Policy

While the Japanese as a nation have few illusions about the Soviet presence and potential threat in the Asian-Pacific region, they have reacted negatively to the stridency of Reagan's anti-Soviet views. Most Japanese see little wisdom in the President's calling the Soviet Union "the focus of evil in the modern world" or his linking a plea for strategic defense to a major speech on military spending.[44] As one article put it: What we want to hear from President Reagan, among other things, is concerned with what measures he has prepared for resolving the U.S.-Soviet deadlock. . . . "[45] Short of this, the stress on alleged Soviet perfidy could only "spawn a futile arms race."

As noted, the Japanese clearly recognize the potential Soviet threat to Japan, but many believe that threat is exaggerated.[46] The Chairman of the Foreign Affairs Research Council of Japan's leading Liberal Democratic Party (LDP) has argued as follows:

> Within Japan, the idea of how they want the Soviet Union to be and how the Soviet Union actually is is greatly mixed up. . . . I am one of the people who think that the Soviet Union is a threat . . . [but] it is necessary to make efforts to open the road to the Soviet Union, seizing every possible opportunity.[47]

While the Japanese security debate seems to be emphasizing the defense side of the defense-diplomacy equation, the LDP leader was echoing his countryman's conviction that diplomacy remained crucial in dealing with Moscow.

---

[42] *Asahi Shimbun*, March 28, 1983.
[43] *Tokyo Shimbun*, March 25, 1983.
[44] Ibid.
[45] Ibid.
[46] *Nihon Keizai Shimbun*, March 28, 1983.
[47] Ibid.

Concluding Remarks

Accounts based on newspapers and official statements for both China and Japan reflect, of course, only part of the total picture. In my own discussions with Japanese and Chinese, I have found considerable interest in the technologies and politics of strategic defense. Some of the best qualified specialists in both countries have delved into the U.S. debates on the subject and have begun to worry about the consequences for either success or failure of the announced American program. Makoto Momoi, formerly a professor at the Japan Defense College and now a research fellow at *Yomiuri Shimbun*, has characterized this worry as follows:

> One of the problematic points of the Reagan strategy is that it has given the impression that first consideration is given to the security of the U.S.[48]

He argues that the United States "will not be able to defend its allies against a nuclear war or against a limited war." The result is "the U.S. capability for crisis management as a superpower has declined." Similarly, Chinese specialists whom I have met in Beijing and at the Stanford Center for International Security and Arms Control have begun to probe the complexities of strategic defense and the possible meaning of the program for the PRC's small retaliatory nuclear forces. Such interest is still sporadic and unofficial, but few Chinese or Japanese who have begun the quest for greater understanding of President Reagan's Strategic Defense Initiative express any confidence that the security interests of their countries will carry much weight in U.S. planning as the program proceeds.

[48] *Yomiuri Shimbun*, May 7, 1983.

Index

Abalakova, 19
ABM-X-3 system, 19
ABM
  and allies, 12, 75–79, 95
  costs, 3, 25
  destabilizing effects, 2–3, 15–16,
    22–23, 29–38, 82–91, 95–96
  effectiveness, 14–15
  feasibility, 24–25
  futility of, 2
  launchers, 9–10, 88
  and radar, 9–10
  and sensors, 40, 85, 99
  and Soviet Union, 4, 13–15, 18–22, 26,
    72–79, 94
  vulnerability, 25
  see also ABMT; SDI
ABM Treaty (ABMT), 86, 87–91
  agreed statements, 9–10, 89, 123–124
  and allies, 74–75, 77
  Article I, 7–8, 118
  Article II, 9–10, 118
  Article III, 8, 118–119
  Article V, 8–9, 11, 21–22, 24, 25, 89,
    98, 119
  Article VI, 9, 19, 89, 98, 119
  Article IX, 89, 94, 120
  Article XIII, 10, 13, 90, 98, 121
  Article XIV, 10, 121
  common understandings, 124–126
  and China, 78–79, 136–137
  deployment restrictions, 8, 11–12, 31,
    33
  and deterrence, 82, 87, 96–97
  "development" restrictions, 8, 10–11,
    31, 33

duration, 7, 122
  effectiveness, maintaining, 87–91, 97
  and hard-site defense, 9, 70
  modification, 99
  number of missiles restrictions, 8, 19
  preamble, 12, 34, 35, 85, 117–118
  protocol to, 129–131
  radar restrictions, 9, 19–20, 22, 88, 91,
    99, 118–119
  research and development restrictions,
    11, 91
  SDI effects on, 6, 7–13, 90–91, 95,
    98–99
  SDI violations of, 24, 25, 94, 96
  and sea-based missiles, 8, 10, 24, 119
  and Soviet Union, 4, 13–17, 87–91;
    see also Breakout
  and space-based missiles, 8–9, 10, 11,
    24, 25, 119
  and strategic relations stability, 29–38,
    85–91, 96–97
  and terminal defense, 96
  testing restrictions, 8, 21–22, 98
  text, 117–122
  and thin ABM defense, 71
  unilateral statements, 126–128
  verification of, 9, 11, 89–90, 98
Accidental nuclear war, 17, 68
  measures against, 30
  and thin ABM defense, 70–72
Aerosol defense against lasers, 50
Agreed Statement D, 9–10, 89
Agreement on the Prevention of Nuclear
  War (1978), 15, 36, 37
Air-based missiles
  and ABMT restrictions, 8–9, 10, 24

Airborne Optical Systems (AOS), 111
Allies
  and ABMs, 12, 75–79, 95
  and SDI, reaction to, 4–5, 6, 74–79,
    95, 138–142
Andropov, Yuri, 4, 22–24, 27, 37, 84,
  105–106, 134
Antarctica Treaty, 136
Antiballistic missiles. *See* ABM
Antiballistic Missile Treaty. *See* ABMT
Antisatellite weapons, 25
Antisimulation, 59
Antitactical ballistic missile, 85
Arms control
  and ABM, 76–77, 104–141
  and China, 134–135, 136–137
  history of, 32–33
  see also SALT I; SALT II; START
Asahi Shimbun, 140
Atmospheric effects, 56–57, 112
Atomic bomb, Soviet development of, 26
AWST, 47, 48 n. 76, 52, 59

Balance of power and Soviet policy,
  15–16
Baruch plan, 32
*Basic Principles of Relations between the
  USA and the USSR,* 30–31
Basing of SDI defense, 53–54, 94
Batitskii, P.F., 14, 18
Battle management systems, 40, 58-61, 94
  and SDI development program, 109,
    110, 113–114
Bombers, 62, 87, 95, 96
Boost phase, interception during, 12, 40,
  42–58, 61, 71 n. 109, 110, 112
  hybrid concept, 44, 55–57
  and pop-up missiles, 44, 50–55, 60, 63,
    94
Booster rockets, 53–55
  hardening against laser attacks, 44, 46
    n. 72, 48, 49–50
Breakout, 12–13, 19, 21, 22, 72–73, 79,
  84–85
Brezhnev, L.I., 17, 23, 29
Bus, 40, 53, 110

Canada, 12
Catholic bishops, 6, 33–34
Cherednichenko, M., 15

Chernenko, 37–38
Chervov, N., 24, 27
China, 78–79, 133–138
Choson Ilbo, 139 n. 32
CIA, 19
Cloud cover, 56–57
Communications links, 40
  vulnerability, 50, 60, 62
Computers, 21
Convention on Prohibition and
  Restrictions on the Use of Certain
  Conventional Weapons, 137
Cooper, Robert, 58 n. 96, 63
Cruise missiles, 62, 63
  sea-based, 89, 95
  Soviet defense against, 20, 22, 23
  Soviet development of, 27, 86–87

Data handling, 59, 114
"Declaration on Atlantic Relations,"
  77–78
Decoys, 50, 59–60, 110
Defense-in-depth. *See* Layered defense
Defensive Technologies Study, 113, 114
DeLauer, Richard, 3–4, 63, 107–115
Deployment
  ABMT restrictions, 8, 11–12, 31, 33
Deterrence, 31, 37 n. 60, 64–69
  and ABMT, 82, 87, 96–97
  and allies, 77–78
  and strategic stability, 81–82, 96–97
Directed-energy systems, 57–58, 88, 109,
  111–112
  and Soviet Union, 21

Early-warning systems, 19–20, 40
Eisenhower, Dwight D., 32
Euromissiles, 75, 84, 86, 87

First-strike capability, 24, 65–69
Fletcher, James C., 39 n. 63
Fletcher Committee, 47, 48 n. 26, 53 n.
  90, 59 n. 98, 60 n. 100
France, 76–78, 86

Galosh missiles, 18, 86
Geneva Protocol for the Prohibition of the
  Use in War of Asphyxiating, Poisonous
  and Other Gases, 137
Grand Forks ICBM field, 70

144

Grechko, A.A., 16
Gromyko, Andrei, 140
Ground-launched missiles, 44, 60
    European deployment, 75, 84, 86, 87
Guangming ribao, 135–136
Guidance systems, 21

HADS, 8
Hard-site defense program. *See* HSD
Hawk missile, 9
Heat shields, 46 n. 72, 50
Henry, Ernst, 16–17
High-altitude defense system. *See* HADS
High-frontier proposals, 58
Hiroshima, 28
Homing Overlay Experiment (HOE), 8
Hongqi, 134
"Hot line," 30
HSD, 61, 64, 68, 70
    and ABMT restrictions, 9, 70
    and deterrence, 96
Hydrogen-fluoride chemical laser, 45–46
Hypervelocity gun system, 112–113

ICBM sites, 8, 20
    and boost-phase intercept, 47 n. 74
    see also HSD
Interceptor missiles, 12, 18
Interim Offensive Agreement, 34–35, 85
Intermediate-range missiles, 62, 75, 89, 95
International Atomic Energy Agency, 136–137

Japan, 78, 138–142

Keyworth, George, 56 n. 94, 65, 83–84, 86–87
Kiev, 19
Kill fluence, 45–47, 53 n. 90, 57
Kinetic energy weapons, 112–113
Kissinger, Henry, 35
Kohl, Chancellor, 77 n. 112
Kokoshkin, A.A., 24–26
Komsomol'sk-na-Amure, 19
Kosygin, A.N., 2
Krasnoyarsk, 19–20, 22
Krushchev, Nikita, 13–14
Krylov, N.I., 14

Lamberson, Donald, 46, 48–49
Land-based missiles. *See* Ground-based missiles
Lasers, 39
    aiming accuracy, 46–47
    chemical, 44–55, 60
    costs, 48 n. 80, 50
    countermeasures, 44, 48, 49–50
    and defense against ABM, 25, 37
    deployment, 12
    ground-based, 25, 27, 50–57, 60, 111
    hardening against, 27, 44, 46 n. 72, 48, 49–50
    and optical imagery, 111
    power output requirements, 46, 47–48, 56, 114–115
    and sensors, 49, 55
    space-based, 44–52, 111
    x-ray, 50–55, 60, 63
Latin America Nuclear Free Zone Treaty, 137
Launchers, 9–10, 88
Layered defense, 12, 39–42, 65
Leningrad ABM deployment, 14
Liberal Democratic party (Japan), 141
Limited Nuclear Test Ban Treaty (1963), 11, 24
Long Wavelength Infrared (LWIR) sensors, 111

McNamara, R., 17
Malinovskii, R. Ya., 14
Midcourse phase intercept, 40, 42–44, 58–61
    and SDI development program, 110, 111
    and thin defense, 71
Midgetman missile, 70, 82
"Mike" test, 26, 28
Military Encyclopedic Dictionary, 17
Military Strategy (Sokolovskii), 13
Military Thought, 15, 18
Mirrors, 55–57
    see also Optics
MIRVs, 5 n. 5, 28, 40, 63, 94
    and arms control, 85–86
MIRVd ICBM, 82
Miscalculation, nuclear war by, 17, 30, 68
    and thin ABM defense, 70–72
Mobile land-based missiles, 96

ABMT restrictions, 8, 9, 119
Momoi, Makoto, 142
Moscow, ABM deployment, 2, 14, 18–19, 72, 73
Moscow Summit, 30–32, 87
  communique, 34–35
Multiple independently targeted reentry vehicle. *See* MIRVs
Mutual destruction, 30–31
MX program, 66
  and Soviet Union, 23, 84–85

Nakasone, Prime Minister, 139 n. 35, 140
National Air Defense Forces (Soviet Union), 13
National Tri-Service Laser Test Range, 111
NATO, 66, 74–78, 95
Nixon, Richard M., 2, 10–11, 35
Nonstrategic missiles systems
  and Soviet Union, 19, 22
  upgrading for ABM, 9–10, 20, 22, 62, 89
North Atlantic Assembly, 74–75
Nth nuclear powers, 64, 70–72, 79
Nuclear explosions
  and countermeasures, 50, 59
  and dust-cloud defense, 70
  and x-ray lasers, 51–55, 111
Nuclear freeze movement, 6, 33–34
Nuclear weapons in space, limitations on, 11

Offensive-defensive strategy, 15–16, 32, 69–70
Ogarkov, N.V., 17, 67
Optics, 45–46, 55–57, 94, 111, 112
  active, 56–57
  vulnerability, 49, 57, 60
Outer Space Treaty, 11, 24, 136
Override command devices, 71–72

Particle beams, 39, 57–58, 111
Patriot missile, 9
Peace movement, 137–138
Pechora, 19–20
Pellet screens, 58, 70
Penetration effectiveness of missiles, 81–82
Pershing II missiles, 62, 137

and NATO, 75
  Soviet response to, 22, 23, 86
Pop-up missile systems, 44, 50–55, 60, 63, 94
Post-boost vehicle. *See* Bus
President's Commission on Strategic Forces. *See* Scowcroft Commission
Pushkino radar, 18

Radar
  ABMT restrictions, 9, 19–20, 22, 88, 91, 99, 118–119
  early warning, 19–20
  mobile, 9, 85
  phased array, 18–19, 57
  research and development, 88–89
  and Soviet Union, 18–20, 22, 85
  upgrading for ABM use, 9
  vulnerability, 18–19
Raman cells, 56
Reagan, Ronald, 1, 3, 4, 7, 40, 101–103
Real-time signal processing, 14
Red-out, 59
Reentry vehicle intercept, 40, 42, 61
  and SDI development program, 110, 111
Renmin ribao, 135, 136, 138
Retroflectors, 25
Research and development, 65, 86–87, 88, 95
  and ABMT, 11, 91
  radar, 88–89
  SDI, 95, 98
  sensors, 88
  Soviet Union, 13, 18–22, 26, 66, 72–73

SA-12 missile, 20, 89
Safeguard ABM system, 70, 86
Sagdeev, R.Z., 24–25
Sakharov, Andrei, 16–17, 24
SALT I, 5, 29–32, 57, 84
  hearings, 10–11
SALT II, 28, 33, 37, 87, 88
SAM
  and ABM upgrading, 9, 20, 22, 62, 89
  Soviet Union, 20, 22
Sanity check, 113
Saryshagan, 21
Satellites

146

number required for SDI, 47–49,
    59 n. 98
vulnerability, 25, 49, 62–63, 74, 83
SCC, 10, 13, 22, 85, 90, 98, 121
Scheer, Robert, 26
Scowcroft Commission, 11 n. 8, 63, 66,
    81–82, 91
SDI
    and ABMT, effects on, 6, 7–13, 90–91,
        95, 98–99
    and ABMT, violations of, 24, 25, 94, 96
    and allies, 4–5, 6, 74–79, 95, 138–142
    and battle management, 109, 110, 113–
        114
    costs, 3, 25, 93, 98, 108–109
    countermeasures, 27–28, 44, 46 n. 72,
        48, 49–50, 94
    demonstration schedule, 111, 112
    destabilizing effects, 22–23, 29–30,
        64–70, 84, 93, 94–95
    management of, 108
    power requirements, 46, 47–48, 56,
        114–115
    research and development, 95
    sharing of technology, 26–27, 90
    Soviet reactions to proposal, 4, 22–27,
        66, 82–91
    Soviet response options, 66–70
    and START negotiations, 5, 95, 99
    and strategic relations, 5–6, 22–23,
        29–38, 63–70, 81–91, 93, 95–96
    support programs, 109, 114–115
    systems analyses, 113–114
    technical feasibility, 4, 24–25, 39–63,
        93–94, 110–115
    testing, 94, 98, 111, 112
    vulnerability, 18–19, 25, 27, 49, 57, 60,
        62–63, 74, 83
Sea-based missiles, 62
    ABMT restrictions, 8, 10, 24, 119
    cruise missiles, 89, 95
    see also SLBM
Semeiko, Lev, 24
Sensors, 8, 40, 91
    ABM, 40, 85, 99
    early warning system, 40
    infrared, 111
    and laser systems, 49, 55
    research and development, 88

vulnerability, 49, 50, 59, 62
    and terminal defense, 61
Sentinel ABM, 71
Sentry missile, 9
SH-04 missile, 18, 19, 21–22
SH-08 missile, 18, 19, 21–22
SLBM, 20, 76, 82, 85
    and deterrence, 96
    and SDI program, 110
    see also sea-based missiles
Smith, Gerard, 10–11, 15
Software, 21, 59–60, 114
Sokolovskii, V.D., 13, 14, 15
South Korea, 139
Soviet Military Power (DOD), 25 n. 43
Soviet Union
    and ABM, 4, 13–15, 18–22, 26,
        72–79, 94
    and ABMT, 4, 13–27, 87–91
    and arms control, 83–84
    and cruise missile, 27, 86–87
    and NATO, 75–78
    research and development, 13, 18–22,
        26, 66, 72–73
    and SALT I, 14, 15–17, 28–39
    and SAM, 20, 22
    and SDI, reaction to proposal, 4,
        22–27, 66, 82–91
    and SDI, response options, 27–29,
        66–70
Space-based missiles
    ABMT restrictions, 8–9, 10, 11, 24, 25,
        119
    and boost-phase intercept, 44–50
    feasibility, 24–25
    vulnerability, 25, 27
Space mines, 25, 27, 49, 60
Sprint missile, 18
Sputnik I, 28, 134
SS-18 ICBM, 20, 27, 46 n. 72
SS-20, 62, 75, 138
Stalin, Josef, 26
Standing Consultative Committee.
    See SCC
START, 33, 73–74, 87
    and ABM, 83, 85–86
    and SDI, 5, 95, 99
Statement on the President's Strategic
    Defense Initiative (DeLauer), 3–4
Strategic bombers. See Bombers

147

Strategic Defense Initiative. *See* SDI
Strategic Defense Technology Office, 109
Strategic relations with Soviet Union
   and ABM, 2–3, 15–16, 22–23, 29–38,
      82–91, 95–96
   and ABMT, 29–38, 85–91, 96–97
   and SDI, 5–6, 22–23, 29–38, 63–70,
      81–91, 93, 95–96
Submarine-launched ballistic missiles.
   See SLBM
Surface-to-air missiles. *See* SAM

Tactical nuclear weapons, 89
Talenskii, N., 14
Tanikawa, Kazuo, 138–139
Tate, Grayson D., Jr., 7, 8
Teller, Edward, 27–28, 50 n. 84
Terminal defense, 61, 71, 96
Thin ABM defense, 64, 70–72
Threshold Test Ban Treaty (1974), 52
Trident missile, 19, 82, 84
   D-5, 23

United Kingdom, 12, 76, 77–78, 86
U.N. Commission on Disarmament, 137
U.S. Air Force Space Command, 134
U.S. Congress, House, Committee on
   Armed Services, 3–4
U.S. Congress, Senate, Armed Services
   Committee, 10–11
U.S. Department of Energy, 114
Ustinov, D.F., 23

Velikhov, E., 26

Wang Shu, 137
Warheads, 59–60
Warner, John, 60 n. 99
Weinberger, Caspar, 23, 77 n. 112, 109
West Germany, 77 n. 112
White Sands Missile Range, N.M., 111
Woerner, Manfred, 77 n. 112

Xinhua, 134, 135
X-ray lasers, 50-55, 50, 63

Zemskov, V.M., 15–16

About the Authors

Sidney D. Drell is Co-Director, Center for International Security and Arms Control, and Professor and Deputy Director, Stanford Linear Accelerator Center. He received his B.A. from Princeton University and his M.A. and Ph.D. in theoretical physics from the University of Illinois.

Since 1960, Dr. Drell has been active as an adviser to the executive and legislative branches of government on technical issues related to national security and defense. He served as a member of the President's Science Advisory Committee and has been a consultant to the National Security Council and the U.S. Arms Control and Disarmament Agency. In 1978 and 1980, he headed studies on MX missile basing for the Pentagon (under the auspices of the JASON Division). He is a director of the Arms Control Association in Washington, D.C., and a member of the National Academy of Sciences and the American Academy of Arts and Sciences.

Philip J. Farley is a Senior Research Associate at the Center for International Security and Arms Control. He served in the United States government for over thirty years, working in the Department of the Air Force, the Atomic Energy Commission, the Department of State, and the Arms Control and Disarmament Agency (ACDA). He dealt principally with international security affairs, arms control, and international scientific cooperation in security-related areas such as atomic energy and outer space. During the first Nixon Administration, from 1969 to 1973, he was Deputy Director of ACDA and Alternate Chairman of the U.S. delegation to the SALT I negotiations.

David Holloway is also a Senior Research Associate at the Center for International Security and Arms Control. He is on a three-year leave from the University of Edinburgh, where he holds the position of Reader in Politics. He received his M.A. and Ph.D. degrees from the University of Cambridge.

A specialist on the Soviet Union, Dr. Holloway conducts research primarily on arms control and defense policy and on the relationship between science and politics. He has written extensively on the operations of the Soviet defense sector and Soviet military technology. He is currently working on a study examining the technological, organizational, military, and political aspects of Soviet nuclear policy from 1939 to 1955.

Members, Center for International Security and Arms Control
Stanford University

Elie Abel, Professor, Communication
Herbert L. Abrams, Professor, Radiology, Harvard Medical School
Lew Allen, Director, Jet Propulsion Laboratory
John H. Barton, Professor, School of Law
Randy Bean, Independent Producer
Barton J. Bernstein, Professor, History
David Bernstein, Consultant, Center
Coit D. Blacker, Senior Research Associate and Associate Director, Center
Paul Brown, Assistant Associate Director, Lawrence Livermore National
    Laboratory
Claude A. Buss, Professor Emeritus, History
Warren Christopher, Partner, O'Melveny and Meyers
Alexander Dallin, Professor, History
Sidney Drell, Professor and Deputy Director, Stanford Linear Accelerator Center;
    Co-Director, Center
Gloria Duffy, Consultant, MacArthur Foundation
Donald Dunn, Professor, School of Engineering
Rob Elder, Editor, San Jose *Mercury News*
David Elliott, Vice President, Research and Analysis Division, SRI International
Alain C. Enthoven, Professor, Graduate School of Business
Jack Evernden, Research Geophysicist, U.S. Geological Survey
Philip J. Farley, Senior Research Associate, Center
Thomas Fingar, Senior Research Associate, International Strategic Institute at
    Stanford
Alexander L. George, Professor, Political Science
Sidney Graybeal, Vice President, System Planning Corporation
David Holloway, Senior Research Associate, Center
Ryukichi Imai, Ambassador for Japan to the United Nations Committee on
    Disarmament
Gerald W. Johnson, Senior Staff Engineer, TRW, Inc.
Thomas Johnson, Lt. Colonel, U.S. Military Academy, West Point
Lynn Joiner, Producer, *Foreign Exchange*, KQED-FM, San Francisco
Donald Kennedy, President, Stanford University
Marjorie Kiewit, Consultant, Center
Hiroshi Kimura, Professor, Slavic Research Center, Hokkaido University, Japan
Joshua Lederberg, President, Rockefeller University
Elliott Levinthal, Professor, School of Engineering

John W. Lewis, Professor, Political Science, and Co-Director, Center
Gerald J. Lieberman, Vice Provost; Dean, Graduate Studies and Research; Professor, School of Engineering
Joseph Martin, Partner, Pettit and Martin
Michael M. May, Associate Director at Large, Lawrence Livermore National Laboratory
Masashi Nishihara, Professor, National Defense Academy, Japan
Hisahiko Okazaki, Ambassador, Ministry of Foreign Affairs, Japan
Daniel I. Okimoto, Assistant Professor, Political Science, and Co-Director, Northeast Asia–United States Forum on International Policy
Nancy Okimoto, Associate Chairman, International Strategic Institute at Stanford
Wolfgang K. H. Panofsky, Professor and Director, Stanford Linear Accelerator Center
M. Elisabeth Paté-Cornell, Assistant Professor, School of Engineering
William Perry, Executive Vice President and Managing Director of Technology, Hambrecht and Quist
Theodore J. Ralston, Representative, International Liaison Office, Microelectronics and Computer Technology Corporation
Condoleezza Rice, Assistant Professor, Political Science, and Assistant Director, Center
Kiichi Saeki, Senior Advisor, Nomura Research Institute, Japan
James J. Sheehan, Professor, History
Motoo Shiina, Member of the House of Representatives, National Diet, Japan
Lawrence Smith, John F. Kennedy School of Government, Harvard University
Robin Staffin, Staff Member, Lawrence Livermore National Laboratory
Adlai Stevenson, Counselor, Mayer, Brown and Platt
Strobe Talbott, Head, Washington Bureau, *Time*
Robert E. Ward, Professor, Political Science
Edward L. Warner III, Senior Research Staff, Rand Corporation
J. Fred Weintz Jr., Partner, Goldman, Sachs and Co.
Albert D. Wheelon, Vice President, Space and Communications Division, Hughes Aircraft Corporation
John A. Wilson, Senior Partner, Wilson, Sonsini, Goodrich and Rosati